Command-Train
Your Dog

COMMAND-TRAIN YOUR DOG

*foolproof obedience techniques
for home and show*

JAMES GORDON BENNETT

A SPECTRUM BOOK

PRENTICE-HALL, INC., Englewood Cliffs, New Jersey 07632

Library of Congress Cataloging in Publication Data

Bennett, James Gordon
  Command-train your dog.

  Includes index.
  1. Dogs—Training. 2. Dogs—Obedience trials.
I. Title.
SF431.B425   636.7′08′3   79-21672
ISBN 0-13-152629-4
ISBN 0-13-152611-1 pbk.

PHOTOGRAPHS BY GREGORY GORE

© 1980 by PRENTICE-HALL, INC.,
Englewood Cliffs, N.J. 07632
A Spectrum Book

Printed in the United States of America

10 9 8 7 6 5 4 3 2 1

Cover design by Infield/D'Astolfo Associates
Manufacturing buyer: Barbara Frick

Prentice-Hall International, Inc., *London*
Prentice-Hall of Australia Pty. Limited, *Sydney*
Prentice-Hall of Canada, Ltd., *Toronto*
Prentice-Hall of India Private Limited, *New Delhi*
Prentice-Hall of Japan, Inc., *Tokyo*
Prentice-Hall of Southeast Asia Pte. Ltd., *Singapore*
Whitehall Books Limited, Wellington, *New Zealand*

About the Author

Jim Bennett has had years of experience in handling, showing, and training dogs. He has been a teacher, training director, and programmer of the dog training classes in the Ridgewood Community School.

As director of the Ridgewood Community School, I saw Jim build our dog training program so that the number of weekly classes increased from two to six. The program was also expanded so that it included instructions in the Beginner's, Novice, Open, and Utility Courses.

The best evidence of Jim's ability to teach others can be found in the words of the dog owners he trained at our school. "Insight," "knowledge," "warmth," "patience," and "understanding" are some of the qualitites attributed to Jim by his former students. As one dog owner put it, "He combines both discipline and compassion in his handling of each dog. This makes him a truly excellent instructor."

One of Jim's satisfied students brought his work to the attention of Prentice-Hall. The publisher agreed that Jim was well qualified and Jim began work on a book that could be read and understood by dog owners of all ages.

It has been my privilege to have been associated with Jim for many years and it has been the school's good fortune to have had him as our training director and programmer.

Raymond J. Murphy
Director, Ridgewood Community School

Contents

Self-Evaluation, 147

**Corrective Actions
for Everyday Problems, 162**

To
Cedarhill Snowblaze Tawny,
A Yellow Labrador Retriever
With a Black Spot,
Who Gave So Much Love and Devotion

Preface

Dog obedience training can be a rewarding and enjoyable pastime. Its rewards are obvious in that you start with a lovable, but undisciplined, animal and your end product is an intelligent, well-behaved member of the household.

The fun part of this process may be a bit more difficult to see. You might have to try working with your dog to appreciate why many people consider obedience training an enjoyable hobby. The simplest explanation of why this experience can be fun is that it allows you to spend several hours with the family pet.

If you decide to train your dog and use this book as a guide, you will learn the commands and exercises that are taught in four different obedience courses—specifically, the Beginner's, Novice, Open, and Utility Classes. Most of this curriculum has a practical value and will increase your dog's ability to learn. By "practical value" I mean that most of the exercises in this book will have an application in your everyday life. For example, you will find it easier to walk with your dog (and more enjoyable) after you have read Chapter 2 and have taught him how to heel.

There are many good books that describe obedience training. To make this volume worth recommending, I have included a few features that I believe are unique:

(1) I have passed along some of the "training tricks" that I have developed in a lifetime of working with dogs.

(2) In the discussion of each exercise I have included at least one paragraph on *corrective action*. This tells you what steps to take if, after you teach an exercise to your dog, he does not respond in the way he should.

(3) Following the presentation of each new exercise there is a sequence of photos that shows the performance of the exercise from beginning to end.

(4) At the end of each chapter there is a judge's worksheet that shows the types of errors that judges look for in a competition. You will find this information helpful even if you have no interest in showing your dog.

(5) Chapter 6 contains five quizzes that are based on the information in the previous chapters. You can test yourself with these quizzes to see how much of the book you remember. Or, if you prefer, you can read the answer section for each quiz to get a convenient summary of each chapter.

(6) The final chapter of the book will show you how to deal with everyday problems. These problems are listed in alphabetical order for easy reference.

While these features may be attractive, the most significant quality of the book is that it really works. I tested it by giving a copy of each chapter to a neighbor of mine who had never worked with dogs. She trained her pet from the manuscript and the two of them progressed at the same rate that I did. In other words, they learned the material in each course in the amount of time it took me to write the next chapter. The success of this couple—handler and dog—is demonstrated throughout the book. They are the models that appear in every photograph.

What this new handler accomplished—and what has been accomplished by most of my students—is also within your reach. You can use this book to *command-train your dog* if you read the description of one exercise at a time and if you then practice that exercise with your dog. It is also necessary to arrange a schedule that calls for daily practice sessions and to plan these sessions according to the suggestions on page 171. Most important, you must remember to be patient and to be generous with your praise. Animals, like humans, perform their best when they receive encouragement.

If you follow these recommendations, you should be successful and you should find obedience training to be both enjoyable and rewarding.

Before concluding this preface I would like to thank Gregory Gore for his fine photography; Linda Stibick and her dog, Duke, for

their appearance in the photos; Raymond J. Murphy, for his intro-
ductory remarks; and Ken Cashman, for helping me to write and
organize this book. Special thanks are also due to Mr. and Mrs. Cliff
Webster for the guidance they gave me when I worked as their assistant.

Jim Bennett

Before Obedience Training Begins

While this is a book about obedience training, it would be a mistake to start this chapter with the teaching of the first command. An owner's responsibility begins long before that. It starts on the day that the family decides that they want to own a dog.

Selecting a puppy, getting ready for his arival, and—like it or not—housebreaking are all part of the owner's job. This chapter will make a few suggestions as to how that job can be done effectively.

SELECTING A DOG

Sometimes, selecting a dog isn't something you do, it's something that happens to you. For example, a neighbor's pet may have a large litter. Your neighbor, being friendly, invites you over to see the puppies. The whole family falls in love with one of the animals and, without any previous consideration, you and your family become dog owners.

Many pets are obtained in this way. With the proper training (the subject of this and later chapters), these dogs may find a happy home.

Much of the time, however, the selection of a pet is a slower and more deliberate process. The best way to start looking for a dog is to hold a family discussion. Find out if everyone wants a dog and if anyone favors a particular breed. The next step should be a trip to the library. There are several books that show pictures of the popular breeds and discuss their characteristics. You and your family should review these books and decide on the type of dog that seems right for your home.

When you make this decision, there are several factors that you should consider. For example, you should ask yourself

Do I want a large dog or small dog?

Do I want a long-haired dog or short-haired dog?

Do I want a dog that requires a lot of exercise? If so, will I have time to walk him adequately?

Do I want to pay for a perfect specimen who will be a show dog or am I only interested in having a family pet?

Once you have answered these questions, I would suggest that you look in the local and out-of-town newspapers to see what prices are being asked for the type of dog you want. If these prices are within your budget, you are ready to start shopping.

There are many places that sell dogs, but my own recommendation is that you try the breeders. Before you look at their dogs, ask for prices. Otherwise, you may become attached to an animal who costs more than you want to spend.

If you know someone who has a knowledge of breeding, it is worththwhile to enlist their help. While this person may charge a fee, he or she will act in your behalf. Once you have selected a pet, your consultant can check its pedigree papers to make sure that its lineage has been traced through at least four generations. The consultant will also make sure that the puppy is not the product of inbreeding or overbreeding. The former term describes the mating of two dogs who are closely related. The offspring of such a pair is likely to be defective. "Overbreeding" indicates that the puppy's mother has been mated too frequently. Conscientious breeders will avoid this. They will mate a female dog during every second or third period of heat. If the bitch is mated more often, her offspring are likely to possess a bad temperament.

Before you leave the breeder with your new dog, you (or your consultant) should examine the dog and should ask the breeder for a guarantee against defect or disease. Along with this guarantee, you should obtain the dog's medical history report and a record of the shots that he has received. Hold onto both of these documents and take them to your veterinarian when your dog is ready for his six-month checkup.

Whether you get your dog from a breeder or from another source, it is not advisable to separate a puppy from its mother until the puppy is at least nine to eleven weeks old. At this age, puppies show signs of independence. They will move into a new home readily and will soon forget their previous surroundings. They have formed some habits in their early days, but their behavior in your house will depend on you.

BRINGING THE PUPPY HOME

Your dog's first day at home will be an exciting event for the entire family. Everyone will want to play with the new pet. The puppy will enjoy this attention. But, at the same time, he will be sniffing around to become familiar with his new surroundings. While the puppy is learning about his home, he must also learn how to live with you and your family. A type of informal training program should begin on the first day. To make this training successful, some advance preparation is required.

The first thing to do is to select a place where you will want your puppy to sleep and eat. This should be a part of the house that can be closed off from the rest of the family. As you will see in the next section, the dog will be easier to housebreak if he is given his own little area.

For this area, you will need to supply four things: a small bed, a soft cushion, a feeding dish, and a water bowl. Make sure that the dish and the bowl are a good size. If they aren't, the dog's food is likely to be spilled and the water bowl will be easy for him to kick over. You might also consider putting a hot water bottle in the puppy's bed. The warmth of the bottle will be a substitute for the dog's mother and may keep him from being lonely and from whining during the night.

The dog's eating and sleeping quarters should not be considered a punishment area. To make this corner of the house seem cheerier to its new inhabitant, you can leave a few toys near the dog's bed. There will be times (at night, especially) when the dog must remain in this area. At other times, the rest of the house need not be "off limits." Your dog will want to wander from room to room. You don't have to discourage this activity, but while your dog is roaming you should be observant.

It is a good idea to find out what type of food your dog has been eating and to have this available for his first day at home. Later on, you can experiment with different foods and different brands. How much to feed your dog depends on his size. Most packaged foods have charts that list recommended portions for each weight class. If you have any doubt about how much your pet should eat, check with the previous owner or call your veterinarian.

In addition to buying pet food, you should prepare for your dog's arrival by going to the butcher and getting a marrow bone. Boil this bone until it is white and hard. Then give it to your dog so he can use it for teething. When he feels the urge to chew, he can bite down on this bone instead of grinding his teeth on your furniture.

This device will help your pet as well as your furnishings. Your dog doesn't know it, but many a well-meaning animal has been put out of its home because its master could not keep it from chewing. An early introduction to the marrow bone should eliminate this problem. One word of caution, however, is that you should be careful in the selection of the bone. Avoid steak, chicken, or pork bones, or any other bone that could splinter and get caught in your dog's throat or intestines.

Two other items that should be at your home ahead of the dog are a soft nylon choke collar and a six-foot leash. Some people prefer the conventional dog collar, but this writer feels that the *proper* use of the choke collar and short leash is more effective for housebreaking dogs. The choke collar should be three to four inches longer than your dog's neck. This will allow room for growth and will make the collar easy to slip on and off. The leash should be no wider than one-quarter inch. If later on, the puppy starts to chew on the leash, you may have to replace it with a chain.

There is a right and wrong way to put on the choker. To visualize the correct method, imagine the you are standing to the side of your dog with your left leg next to his right side. If in this position you release the lead, the choker ring should fall to the ground. You can practice this by putting the choker on your left wrist and by pulling the lead with your right hand. Once again, as you release the lead, the choker ring should drop.

Some people feel that it is cruel to put a choke collar on a very young dog, but my experience contradicts this. The nylon collar will not hurt the puppy if it is put on right. The use of the collar and leash will help you to train your puppy in much less time.

If you are preparing a list of the things you will need for your dog's homecoming, these are the items that you should include:

(1) clean area

(2) bed and cushion

(3) food dish and water bowl

(4) toys for the puppy

(5) dog food

(6) a hard marrow bone

(7) nylon choke collar

(8) a six-foot leash.

The time to do your shopping is before the dog comes home. This will allow you to establish your household routines on the first day. It will also spare you from having to run to the store at a time when you want to get acquainted with your pet.

Putting on the Choke Collar

The right way. When the choke collar is released, the choker ring will move counterclockwise around the dog's neck.

The wrong way. Note that when the choke collar is released, the ring will move up and the collar will tighten around the dog's neck.

There is no reason to delay the start of this training. Nor is there any reason to dread it. Housebreaking is not difficult; it just requires a good method and perserverance. In other words, once you select a procedure you should stick with it. Don't get discouraged and don't be forgetful and skip a day. This general rule applies to all phases of animal training.

To describe the housebreaking system that I prefer, let me suggest a 24-hour schedule for a pet that is being trained. In my mind, the training cycle begins at night. The last person to go to bed should take the dog outside and should keep it out until the dog has relieved itself. After this outing, the dog should be put in its sleeping area and should be attached to a stationary object by means of its leash. The leash should be shortened to prevent the dog from wandering away from his bed. This will also minimize the chance of an accident, because a dog will seldom soil the area in which it sleeps and eats.

The choice of a sleeping and eating area was mentioned in the last section. Usually, either the bathroom or the kitchen is preferred. If you select one of these places, the dog can be leashed to a radiator, a sink, or the leg of a sturdy table. This technique should work for you if you remember two things: (1) The dog should not be given any food or water after his last trip outside. (2) The dog should not be kept on the leash for so long that he cannot restrain himself. What I suggest is that you increase his leash time by a few minutes each night until you can safely leave him for a period of eight hours.

If you are the first person up in the morning, take the dog off the leash and *carry* him outside. By carrying the dog, you will discourage him from messing before he gets to the door. This is important in the morning because after a long night on the leash a young puppy will not have much control. Another reason for carrying the dog is that it gives you a chance to put him down in the same place every time. After several visits to the same area, the dog will learn that this is the spot where he is expected to relieve himself.

Once the dog has urinated and moved his bowels, he should be praised and given an opportunity to play. This play period serves two purposes. It rewards the dog for not having soiled the house and it provides him with some necessary exercise. How long the dog remains outside will depend on his companion's schedule. When it is time to go in, the dog should be returned to his eating and sleeping area and should be given his first meal.

You should repeat the trips outside after every meal and before bedtime. If you feed your puppy four times a day, his number of daily trips (including the early morning and late evening outings) should be no less than six. This means that you will take him out about every 2½ hours. If you find that he can't last for that long, you can add an extra outing.

When the dog is not outside, you should keep him off leash but in his own area. Only use the leash at night or when no one is home. This should be safe because your dog is relieving himself every few hours. If he does have an accident, don't get discouraged and don't interrupt the training.

Each day you should try to add a few minutes to the interval between outings. As your dog becomes accustomed to this routine, you can allow him to roam through the house. Soon he will be giving you signals when he is ready to get out. He may pace back and forth, he may walk around in circles, or he may scratch the door. When you can depend on your dog to let you know that it's time to go out, most of the job is done.

You must still determine if it is safe to stop using the leash at night. To find this out, try one night without the leash followed by one night with the leash on. If this experience is successful, try going two nights in a row without the leash. Continue to alternate—off and on—until you are confident that the lesson has been learned.

When your dog has been housebroken, you should be proud of your pet and proud of yourself. The next big step in your dog's education is the start of obedience training. This should not take place until your pet is housebroken and is almost five months old.

Obedience Training
for Beginners

Everyone recognizes the need for an obedient pet. A dog who doesn't mind his owner, who barks without reason, who soils the house and ruins the furniture is more of a nuisance than a pleasure. There is no argument about that. Where there is room for disagreement, however, is in selecting a method of training—in deciding how you can make your dog more obedient. Should you wait for him to misbehave and then try to correct him? Or should you subject him to a formal training program either at home or in a school. Both approaches are valid and both are presented in this book.

If you are interested in the first approach, you will want to read Chapter 7, which describes the various problems confronting the person who owns a dog. For convenience, these problems have been given titles (such as "Barking," "Gumming," or "Chasing cars") and have been listed in alphabetical order. The description of each problem is followed by a recommended solution.

If you read this chapter and provide no other formal training for your dog, you are following what I call the "troubleshooting" approach. This approach is practical in that it deals only with the problems at hand and is much less time-consuming than a formal course in dog obedience. However, there are advantages to mixing some formal training with the problem-solving techniques. The following example will demonstrate what I mean.

Suppose your newspaper is delivered every day by a youngster on a bicycle. Your dog becomes attracted to the bicycle and makes a habit of chasing the carrier down the street. This continues for a few days until you decide that it's time for corrective action. The next time the youngster arrives, you are armed with a water pistol that contains a mixture of water and vinegar. As your dog starts his pursuit, you squirt a few drops into his mouth. He is not injured, but he is so stunned that he stops running.

After a few days when the newspaper is delivered, your dog will remain at your side. He has learned his lesson. But while he is standing next to you, he sees a cat in the neighbor's front yard. Before you can stop your dog, he runs across the street and is almost hit by a car.

The moral of the story is that problem-solving by itself is not enough. Your dog's life is not as varied as your own, but you can never anticipate every situation that he may face. Thus, you can teach him not to chase a bicycle, but that will not prevent him from running after a cat. There is only one way to protect your pet as new situations arise. You have to be able to communicate with him and get him to understand and obey your commands. While this isn't easy, it can be accomplished if you do the exercises in this chapter and in Chapter 3.

To return to the episode with the bicycle and the cat, let us suppose that you and your dog have had daily training sessions. You have taught your dog the command "stay" and you have practiced with him until his response is automatic. Despite this training, your dog still wants to chase after the bicycle, and corrective action is needed to break him of that habit. When your dog starts to pursue the cat, you shout out the command "stay." Your dog responds—as he has done in practice—by halting immediately. You have stopped him before he has reached the street.

While this story is hypothetical, it is not unlike many other stories that are true. A few years ago my own dog was lured out of the yard by a well-meaning neighbor. As my dog started across the road, I was terrified by the sight of a truck that was speeding toward her. I gave her the command we had used in practice and without hesitation she froze in place. Had she been slow to respond and taken one or two more steps, it is likely that she would have been killed.

There are many other dogs that owe their lives to their obedience training. So it could be argued that one reason for doing the exercises in this book is to provide for your dog's safety. This is an important motive, but it is not the only one. As you start to train your dog, you will find that the two of you are developing a common language. When you say words such as "sit," "stay," or "heel," your dog will understand what you want. The more you practice, the more likely it is that he will obey. As a result, a second advantage of formal obedience training is that it allows you to gain greater control over your pet. Because of this control, there are more things that you can do together. You can walk with your dog and not worry about his trying to break away. You can have visitors in your home and not worry about your dog annoying them. You can take your dog off leash and still have a means of regulating his behavior. If it is not clear now how this can be accomplished, it will be apparent when you read the next two chapters. As you learn about each exercise, you will also be told how the exercise can be helpful in your everyday life.

A third benefit that is derived from dog obedience training is that—like human education—it increases the learning ability of the pupil. Thus, the more you teach your dog, the more intelligent he will become. And because of this intelligence, he will be better equipped to benefit from other types of training.

So if someone were to ask you why obedience training is worthwhile, you could reply that the obedience exercises can help you to raise a safer, more obedient, and more intelligent dog. A pet who possesses these qualities is likely to be happy. And his owner is likely to consider him much more of a pleasure than a nuisance.

There is still another advantage of formal obedience training that you cannot appreciate until you have tried some of the exercises that are in this chapter. When you start to teach your dog and you can see him respond, you will experience a great sense of satisfaction. You will be proud of what your dog is able to do and proud of what the two of you have accomplished together.

The best way to describe this feeling is to compare it to the excitement of a child who has just taught his dog to roll over. Once the dog is successful, the child probably considers him the most intelligent pet in the world. At the same time, the child is looking forward to when the dog can perform for the rest of the family. Many of us experienced this when we were younger. However, few of us recognize that our feelings haven't changed. We still enjoy teaching our dogs tricks and we still like to show them off to our families and friends. Obedience training gives us an opportunity to do both. And it has the extra advantage that while we are satisfying our own needs, we are also making our dogs more obedient pets.

As evidence that obedience training can be fun, there are several thousand dog clubs in the United States whose members have made obedience training their hobby. These people work regularly with their dogs to prepare them for competitions. You may not be interested in entering your dog in a show, but the fact that so many people find this work enjoyable should certainly be encouraging.

THE FIRST COURSE
IN OBEDIENCE TRAINING

When I spoke about formal training in the introduction, I was referring to the commands and exercises that are taught in obedience classes. These classes are generally offered by dog clubs or by schools of continuing education. Obedience work is divided into four different levels. The curriculum for each level is standardized throughout the United States and many other nations. This means that the same exercises are taught regardless of where a class is given. Of course, the technique used to teach an exercise may vary with the instructor.

The first level of obedience work—known as the Subnovice or Beginner's Course—is designed for dogs who have had no previous obedience training. To enter the course, a dog should be close to six months of age and must be housebroken. The class consists of eight to ten hours of instruction. When the course is completed, the dog should be able to perform six fundamental exercises while still on leash.

All of the exercises that are included in the Beginner's Course are presented in this chapter. The methods of teaching these exercises to your dog have been outlined in an original way that will make them easy to learn. If after you have practiced with your dog he is still having a specific problem (if he is not able to perform an exercise in the proper way), you may be able to resolve this by referring to the sections on corrective action.

Thus, from reading this book you should be able to train your dog. However, there are some good reasons for attending a class if you have the opportunity. One advantage is that you can work with your dog in front of an instructor. This way if you do something wrong, your instructor can call it to your attention.

Another advantage is that your dog will learn to obey your commands in the presence of other animals. This is important. For most dogs, there is no greater distraction than the company of other canines. If you can train your pet to resist this distraction, you can be confident of his behavior in almost any situation.

If you do enroll in a course, you will find this chapter a helpful supplement. You can read it in between classes to review what you have learned in school. You can use it as a guide for conducting your own practice sessions. And you can also use it as a reference that contains some helpful techniques that may not have been suggested by your instructor.

PREPARATION FOR
OBEDIENCE TRAINING

To start obedience training, a dog must be housebroken and must have received a shot for rabies. I would begin training when the dog is 4½ months old. However, some instructors will not accept a pet until it is at least a month and a half beyond that age.

If you are taking your dog to class, remember not to give him food or water for a few hours before the class begins. Otherwise, your dog may have difficulty in restraining himself. Nothing embarrasses an owner more than having to clean up after a dog in class.

Only two pieces of equipment are required for obedience training. You will need the leash and the choke collar that were described in the first chapter. The leash should be six feet long and should be made of strong nylon, leather, or canvass. The width of the leash will depend on the size of your dog. If he is no bigger than the average miniature poodle, a one-quarter-inch leash will be sufficient. If he is a large dog, you may need a leash that is as wide as three-quarters of an inch.

Before the start of training, practice putting the choke collar on your dog. If you don't recall how this should be done, please refer to the first chapter. If your dog is not accustomed to wearing a collar, get him used to it before training begins.

You, the handler, can wear whatever is comfortable, but avoid wearing shoes that have an elevated heel. This type of shoe will cause your feet to tire quickly and, more important, it may cause you to lose your balance. If your dog changes directions suddenly, there is a good chance that you will fall.

THE ROLE OF THE HANDLER

The handler and the dog are a team. In competition, they are evaluated on the way they work together. Much of the success of the team is dependent on the handler's ability to communicate with the dog.

In the Beginner's Course, there are four ways in which you, the handler, can influence the behavior of your pet. You can control his actions by using the choke collar and the leash—a method that will not be available to you in later courses. You can also communicate with your dog by altering your tone of voice, by giving him signs of approval, and by means of your general attitude. These four methods will be explored in this section.

13

(1) *The Use of the Choke Collar.* Every exercise begins with the dog in the heel position—that is, the exercise starts with the dog on your left side and with his right front leg aligned and parallel with your left leg. You should fold the loose end of the lead and hold it in your right hand. This way it won't drag on the floor where you can trip over it. Your left hand should also be on the leash about eight to ten inches away from the choke collar. This is the hand that you will use for corrective action.

If your dog starts to misbehave, move your left hand closer to your dog so that there is some slack in the leash. Then quickly snap your hand back so that the leash becomes taut and the dog feels a sharp snap on his collar.

You can repeat this action until your dog responds. How hard you should pull depends on the size of your pet. For large dogs, firm, hard tugs are needed. For smaller pets, you can be a little more gentle. If you are a beginning student, however, you are likely to be less forceful than you should be. You don't want to hurt your dog, but you shouldn't be timid when you pull the leash.

One thing worth remembering is that the palm of your left hand should be turned toward the rear. It should not be facing your body and it should not be pointed in front of you. To understand why, move your left hand as if you are yanking the leash. If your palm is turned to the front or side, the movement of your elbow will be restricted by your body. You will not be able to pull the leash as far or as hard.

(2) *Tone of Voice.* When a dog enters obedience training, he has a very limited understanding of human language. He will increase this understanding in each course, but—at most—his vocabulary will be limited to approximately 50 words. Thus, instructors will tell you not to include a lot of "excess baggage" in your commands. For example, if you want your dog to come, just say "come." Do not say "Come over here, right away!" The words "over here" are superfluous. And the words "right away" should be implied by your tone of voice.

You can also use your tone of voice as a corrective measure. For example, if I work with a dog who misbehaves, I will scold that dog by saying "no" or "shame." These words are uttered in a good firm voice so that the dog understands that I am displeased. If I want to emphasize the point, I will pull the leash at the same time that I reprimand the dog. After I do this a few times, the dog knows to respond to these words and the tug on the choke collar becomes unnecessary.

There is a lesson to be learned from this experience. When you speak to your dog what you say is not as important as the way you say it.

(3) *Showing Signs of Approval.* The first two methods are applied to discourage undersirable behavior. This is a necessary part of obedience training. However, encouragement is necessary too. Students who have worked with me know that I conclude every exercise with the instruction "Praise your dog!" Dogs need to know that they've done well. A gentle pat and a sincere "good boy" or "good girl" will do the job.

(4) *General Attitude.* Your attitude as a handler will be recognized by your dog and will affect his performance. If he knows that you don't like to correct him, he will try to do things his way and will fare badly. On the other hand, if you offer him discipline but no encouragement, he will probably obey you but he will lack enthusiasm. This is significant shortcoming. I have found that the dogs who perform the best are the ones who are eager to please their handlers.

To get the best responses from your dog, try to both firm *and* friendly. Avoid being lenient or permissive, but don't be afraid to show some love and affection.

No two people will handle a dog in exactly the same way. For this reason, it is better to have just one person work with a dog while he is learning the beginning exercises. If you are the one who is training your pet, you will have to discourage the rest of the family from taking a turn.

TEACHING YOUR DOG TO SIT AND STAY (THE LONG SIT)

While this is not the first item on the judge's worksheet, it is a good exercise to choose for the start of practice. There are two reasons why: (1) Since it is easy to learn, it will not be overly taxing for the inexperienced dog and handler. (2) It will provide the dog with a skill that will be helpful for the rest of his training. Once your dog has learned to obey the command "sit," you can use it whenever you need to gain his attention.

You will be glad that your dog has learned this exercise when you have visitors in your home. Many dogs tend to be overly friendly and pounce upon an unsuspecting guest. Even if this person is a dog lover, he or she may not be prepared for this type of reception. This is especially true if your visitor is wearing good clothes.

To separate your dog from your guest all that you need are the commands "sit" and "stay." Suppose that your pet is standing on his hind legs, embracing (and barking at) the newcomer. Rather than trying to pull your dog away, give him the command "sit." As your pet starts to squat, your visitor can begin to retreat. Naturally, the dog will want to follow, but if you have worked with your pet, you can prevent this. Once you give him the command "stay," your pet will remain in place while your harried visitor will be able to take a seat.

Of course, there are many other ways that you can use this command. One important application of learning to stay was demonstrated in the introduction—when I spoke about controlling your dog so that he wouldn't run into the street.

To make this exercise easier to explain, I have presented "sit" and "stay" separately. Furthermore, I have divided each of these commands into three smaller parts: the *position* (meaning the starting position), the *procedure* (which refers to what you teach your dog), and the *performance* (which describes what is expected of your dog after he learns the exercise). These divisions do not exist in the actual exercise. I have introduced them so you dan digest this material in smaller doses.

POSITION: The dog is at your left in the heel position. Your left hand is off the leash and is ready to be placed on the dog's back. The lead is folded in your right hand and this hand is positioned eight to ten inches away from the choke collar.

PROCEDURE: To teach your dog to sit requires three simultaneous actions. These are:

(1) Raise the leash with your right hand so it is directly above the dog's head and he feels the pressure on the choke collar. As the dog starts to sit, release this pressure by lowering your hand and body.

(2) Put your left hand on the dog's back—as close to the tail as possible—and push down. This is a sensitive spot on young puppies, so you shouldn't push too hard.

(3) Give the command verbally by saying your dog's name and the word "sit."

There are sequels to these actions that should be employed *as soon as your dog sits.*

(1) Use your free left hand (if necessary) to move the dog into the correct sitting position. He should be close to your left side; his back should be straight and his front and hind legs should be aligned.

(2) If the dog lowers his head so that his back is no longer straight, get him to lift his head by gently tugging with your right hand.

(3) Once the dog is in the proper position, he deserves some praise. Compliment him by saying "good dog" and emphasize each word so that he knows that you mean it.

PERFORMANCE: As your dog becomes familiar with this exercise, you will not have to prompt him by pulling the leash with your right hand or by pushing his back down with your left. Once he hears the command, he will assume the correct sitting position.

When you are teaching your dog to sit, don't settle for anything less than the correct position. Keep moving your dog until he is in a straight sit. Then praise him and try the exercise again.

What you don't want to do is to have your dog become accustomed to an improper sitting position. If this occurs, your job will be twice as hard. You will first have to break his bad habit and then teach him the right way to do the exercise. The more times you allow him to sit wrong, the more trouble you will have in breaking his habit.

The perfect sit. The dog is in line with but not touching the handler. The dog's front and hind legs are aligned. His head is up straight.

Crooked sit. The dog is not lined up with the handler. In a dog show, or in a competition or class, there would be a penalty for this type of sit.

Wide crooked sit. The dog is not lined up with the handler and is too far away. The dog would lose points in a show, but would not be disqualified.

Once your dog has learned to sit straight after receiving just a verbal command, he is ready for the next part of the exercise. In this part, he will be expected to retain his sitting position while you walk away from him. The command that you give him is "stay." The exercise is performed as follows:

POSITION: The dog is in a straight sit in the heel position. Your left hand is free and your right hand is holding the loose end of the lead about eight to ten inches from the choke collar. (Note there is both a sitting and standing heel position. In both cases, the dog is at the handler's left and the dog's front feet are lined up and parallel with the handler's feet.)

PROCEDURE: The dog will receive three different signals that will tell him to remain in place.

(1) He will receive the verbal command "stay." This should be issued in a sharp and crisp tone of voice. It is not necessary, or advisable, to add any words to this command. The extra verbiage will just confuse the dog.

(2) When you give the command, move your left hand in front of the dog's face so that your palm is directly in his line of sight. Your palm should be turned to the dog and your fingers should be pointing down. Be careful not to hit or touch the dog with this hand, but don't be afraid to place it close to his face.

(3) Now that you've told your dog to stay, start off on your right foot and move away from him. It is important that you remember which foot to step with first. If you make a mistake and start with your left, the dog may think that you want him to heel and he may walk along with you.

Leaving the Dog. When you gave the command, you and your dog were facing in the same direction. Start to walk in this direction until you are separated from your dog by the full length of the leash. At this point, turn around so that you and your dog are facing one another. You are still holding the leash in your right hand. Be careful not to pull it too tight or you will pull the dog out of his straight sitting position.

You and your dog should remain in place for approximately sixty seconds. If you are practicing at home, you can determine when this time has passed. If you are in class, wait for the command from your instructor to "return to your dog."

Return. You have not yet completed the exercise. There is a specific procedure for getting back to the heel position. To begin, cup your left hand and move it over to the leash. When the leash is inside the arc of your hand, close your thumb and forefinger to form a circle. The leash will be pulled through this circle as you are walking back to your dog.

To visualize the path back to your dog, think of the numbers on the face of a clock. Assume that you are standing at six o'clock and you are facing your dog, who is standing at twelve. To get back to the heel position, you must walk to the right (the three o'clock side), while the leash must be kept to the left (the 9 o'clock side). Your right hand reels in the leash as you approach the dog. Your left hand has two functions: (1) It holds the leash on the three o'clock side of the dog and (2) it keeps the slack of the leash from dragging on the floor where it might be a hazard.

When you are along side of your dog, do not stop. At this point, you and your dog are facing in different directions. To correct this, continue walking but gradually turn so that your path forms a semicircle behind the dog. While you are turning, be conscious of the way that you are holding the leash. It should be held aloft so it is not in the dog's eyes. At the same time, it should not be held so tight that the dog is pulled off his sitting position. When you have completed the semicircle, you and the dog will be facing in the same direction. The dog will be at your left in the heel position.

This concludes the exercise. If your dog is still sitting, he deserves your praise. If at any time he has attempted to move, you may have to use corrective action.

PERFORMANCE: The procedure I have just described will still be used after your dog has thoroughly learned this portion of the exercise. The only difference is that you may prefer to use a shorter staying period at the beginning and to work up to a full sixty seconds as your dog gains experience.

It is possible to follow the procedures that I have just outlined and still have trouble with your dog. Sometimes teaching an exercise right is not enough. There are other techniques that are necessary to get your dog to respond. These techniques are known as *corrective actions*. For this exercise, the corrective actions are as follows.

CORRECTIVE ACTIONS: There are two ways in which dogs who are learning to sit and stay can disappoint their handlers. Either the dog can lie down when he's supposed to sit or he can follow the handler when he's supposed to remain in place. If your dog misbehaves in either way, you can use the following technique to help him learn.

(1) The moment your dog leaves the sitting position, scold him by saying "no" and "shame." If you are separated from your dog, return to his side immediately. Make adjustments so that once again he is in a straight sit.

(2) Hold the lead in your left hand about one to two feet away from the choke collar. Repeat the commands "sit" and "stay" and leave the heel position by stepping off with your right foot.

(3) Walk around your dog, counterclockwise, and continue to use the words "sit" and "stay." These should be uttered in a firm tone of voice.

(4) With each rotation gradually lengthen the lead. Continue to do this until you are separated from your dog by the full length of the leash. At this point, stop and turn so that you and your dog are facing one another.

If at any time the dog leaves his sitting position, stop what you are doing and begin the corrective action again.

The left hand tells the dog to stay as the handler takes her first stride with her right foot.

The handler is facing the dog and the two are separated by the full length of the leash.

Returning to the dog. The handler stays to the right of the dog while the leash is kept to the dog's left.

To return to the heel position, the handler walks behind the dog. She must be careful not to dangle the leash in front of the dog's face and not to pull the dog off of his sitting position.

The end of the exercise. The dog is once again in the heel position. This position should be retained until the judge or the person in charge indicates that the exercise is over.

While walking a dog should be a pleasurable experience, there are many people who dread this type of an outing. Their trouble is that they don't have sufficient control over their pets. The person is being "walked" by the dog even though it's the man or woman who is holding the leash.

Have you seen anyone who has this problem? If you have, that person probably resembles one of the fictitious characters described below.

Mr. A has a pet who likes to lag behind and sniff at everything that passes. Mr. A tries to be patient, but after a short while he finds himself tugging on the leash. Despite his efforts, the dog never seems to catch up.

Ms. B has a pet who is constantly overeager. Her dog is not content to walk at the same pace that she does. Instead, the dog keeps running ahead and while Ms. B pulls back on the leash, she has the uncomfortable feeling that she is being dragged.

Mr. C does not enjoy walking his dog because he is constantly prepared for an emergency. He keeps a firm grip on the leash because he knows that any type of distraction will cause his dog to break away.

The purpose of describing these people is not to ridicule them but to point out problems that many people experience. In this exercise, you will learn techniques that will help you to avoid these problems. You will learn how to walk your dog, how to change directions, and how to bring your dog to a complete halt. Some of these techniques will seem familiar because they are closely related to what you learned in the last section.

The first command that you will read about is the word "heel." This tells your dog that he must proceed at your side. After he has learned to obey this instruction, you won't have to worry about his lagging behind, forging ahead, or chasing after another animal. At the first sign of any one of these infractions, you can give him the command and he will return to your side.

To appreciate how well this lesson can be learned, you can look at the photographs at the end of this section. The photographs that show lagging and forging were difficult to take, because our model was so well trained he could not be tricked into walking behind or

24

ahead of his master. Finally, we got him to forge by having him chase a ball while he was still on lead. We were unable to make him lag until near the end of the day when he was getting weary. Before then he was determined to stay at his master's side. If your dog can emulate our model, he will not give you any trouble when you take him for a walk.

POSITION: The dog is at your left and your feet are aligned and parallel with his front feet. The loose end of the leash is folded and held firmly in your right hand. Your left hand is placed on the leash about eight to ten inches from the choke collar. This hand should be positioned so that your palm is turned to the rear.

PROCEDURE: If you are in class, the exercise will start when your instructor says "forward." If you are practicing at home, you can begin whenever you and your dog are ready.

Forward Heel. To get your dog in motion, you must communicate with him in three ways.

(1) You should call his name and give him the command "heel." Pause briefly before issuing the command, so you are sure that you have his attention. As you say the word "heel," make sure that your voice is emphatic.

(2) After you give the command, start to walk in the direction you are facing. Take you first step with your left foot. This is important. As your dog progresses with his training, he will learn to follow you when you start with your left foot and to remain in place when you start with your right.

(3) If your dog does not walk when you do, jerk the lead with your left hand. This should be done as you are taking your first step.

Halt. In class the instructor will say "halt" when it is time for you to stop. If, however, you are on your own, you can choose the time to perform this part of the exercise. Usually, it is a good idea to take twenty to thirty steps and then come to a halt. Your dog will be expected to stop at the same time you do and to assume the sitting heel position. To get him to do this, you can employ three different actions.

(1) Before coming to a halt, take two or three preparatory steps. With each step, your pace should be slowed. This will let the dog know that you are about to make a complete stop.

(2) Once you and your dog are no longer in motion, your dog is expected to sit. If he doesn't, take your left hand off the leash and place it on his back—as close to his tail as possible. With your palm facing down, push the dog into the sitting position.

(3) Move your right hand so that it is six to ten inches away from the choke collar. Pull up on the leash—as necessary—with this hand to keep the dog in a straight sit.

When your dog is learning this part of the exercise, he may require additional prompting. If this is the case, you can give him the command "sit" after you come to a stop. If he does not sit properly, you can use your free left hand to correct his position.

PERFORMANCE: For the forward part of the exercise, you should strive to eliminate item (3)—that is, your dog should follow you when he hears the command "heel" and he sees you take the first step with your left foot. The tugging on the leash should become unnecessary.

Once your dog is trained, he should automatically sit when the two of you come to a stop. You should not have to give him an additional command and you should not have to help him into the correct sitting position.

I would recommend that you practice heeling and sitting for approximately ten minutes before you attempt the about turn. The object of the latter exercise is to turn 180° while the dog continues to heel.

POSITION: The turn is made while the dog is walking at your side in the heel position. You should not come to a stop before changing directions.

PROCEDURE: To reverse directions, always turn to the right and take two steps before completing your turn. By taking these extra steps, you will be turning in an arc instead of doing an abrupt about face. This is important because pivot turns or turns that are very sharp should always be avoided.

When you are teaching the exercise to your dog, you must lead him into the turns by jerking on the leash. As you are changing directions, give the command "heel" so that your dog knows that he must remain in position. Repeat the command any time that your dog seems likely to stray. Do not slow down when you approach a turn. If you do, the dog may think that you are going to stop and he may respond by sitting when you are expecting him to turn.

PERFORMANCE: To make this exercise part of your dog's routine, practice with him twice a day for five minutes each time. When he learns the exercise, he will be able to heel on the turn without any outside help from his handler. In other words, you will not have to give him the command "heel" and you will not have to pull on the leash to keep him from straying.

CORRECTIVE ACTIONS: To develop the proficiency that is described in the performance sections, you will have to practice regularly with your dog. In addition to this training, you may have to concentrate on a specific problem. If you do, refer to the paragraphs below. They offer solutions to some of the most common problems associated with this exercise.

Forward Heel. Some dogs will lie down or refuse to move when they are expected to heel. If your dog behaves in this way, there are two things you should do to correct him. (1) Jerk the lead repeatedly—although not hard—with your left hand. This hand should be positioned about ten to twelve inches away from the choker ring. (2) While you are pulling on the leash, give your dog lots of encouragement. With each tug say "good boy" or "good girl" until your dog begins to move.

Forging, Lagging, and Heeling Wide. When your dog is walking with you there are three ways in which he can go wrong. Instead of walking at your side, he can forge ahead, he can lag behind, or he can swing wide. All of these actions are undesirable. They can usually be corrected by the persistent use of your left hand. What this means is that you will have to tug on the leash until your dog is heeling correctly.

Sometimes the use of the leash is not sufficient. This is particularly true with larger dogs. If you are unable to correct your dog by pulling on the leash, you might try the following technique to keep him from forging.

As your dog is walking in front of you, pull back on the leash with your left hand and pivot on your left foot. Turn 90° so that you are facing into the dog's path. With your right knee bump your dog in the face or nose. A few bumps and a few firm tugs on the leash should be all that is needed to get him to heel correctly.

Another way to improve your dog's heeling is to wrap the lead around your left leg in the vicinity of your knee. With the dog on the shortened lead, take a series of fast steps and then a series of short steps. The purpose of alternating is to get your dog to pay attention. After you repeat this action a few times, your dog will develop the habit of staying close to your left leg.

Failing to Stop and Sit. To correct this problem, bend over and put your right hand on the lead close to the choke collar. In this position, take four or five steps and stop short. When you come to a halt, quickly use your left hand to push the dog into a sitting position. Use your right hand to lift the lead above the dog's head so that he feels the pressure on his choke collar.

As with other corrective measures, this action should be successful if it is frequently repeated. Try doing this four times a day for about a week. At the end of this period, your dog should be able to halt and sit without any extra prompting.

Heeling and About Turn

Following the command "heel," take your first step with your left foot.

Before completing the about turn, take two steps to the right. Avoid making pivot turns, where you and your dog reverse directions abruptly.

Forging. If your dog forges ahead of you, jerk the lead sharply. If necessary, turn into his path and bump him in the chest with your right knee.

Lagging. A good way to eliminate lagging is to take several quick, short steps and then return to your normal pace.

Heeling wide. To discourage this habit wrap the lead around your left thigh so that your dog is kept close to your side. Then alternate between fast and slow heeling.

Halt. If in practice your dog does not sit when you come to a halt, pull up on the leash with your right hand and push down on the dog with your left.

TRAINING YOUR DOG TO HEEL
AND WALK THE FIGURE EIGHT

In the Heeling and About Turn section, you and your dog developed skills that will help you walk together. These skills will be challenged as you start to learn the Figure Eight exercise. You will have to keep your dog at your side as you walk through a very irregular pattern. At the same time, you will have to keep your dog from being distracted as you walk around the posts.

By practicing this exercise, you will accomplish three things: (1) You will reinforce all the skills of heeling (straight heeling, the about turn, and fast and slow heeling). (2) You will teach your dog to follow you even when he cannot anticipate in which direction you are going to turn. And (3) you will train your dog to remain at your side even when something else is competing for his attention.

The third accomplishment requires some explanation. When you begin to practice the figure eight, you can use any two objects to serve as your posts. For example, if you are practicing at home, you might decide to use two chairs. If you are practicing outside, you may be able to work with two trees, two bushes, or two garbage cans. The important thing is that when you approach the post, the dog must not lose his concentration. If he stops heeling and pauses to sniff or examine the post, he is doing the exercise wrong.

Once your dog demonstrates that he can walk around the two objects without being distracted, you should replace the objects with two people. This is the way the exercise is performed in competition. You will find that human posts present a much stiffer challenge because they are a much greater attraction for your dog. He may want to stop and sniff them, brush up against them, or pause to examine them—as he would with a stranger passing on the street. While this behavior is understandable, it must be corrected. You will learn how to do this as you read more of this section. With practice, your dog will learn to devote his attention to you and not to the people who are acting as posts. At the same time, he will learn to heed the person he is walking with and not the poeple who pass him on the street.

After I have taught this exercise to my class, we have had a unique way of performing it. We use dogs instead of people to serve as posts. As you can imagine, this is a difficult test for all the animals involved. Yet, with just a little training, all three dogs (the one doing the exercise and the dogs standing as posts) will perform well.

It is possible to learn this exercise at home without being part of a class. However, it is important that you don't try to do this too soon. Before attempting the figure eight, you should first learn and practice all the aspects of heeling.

POSITION: The exercise begins with the handler and the dog half way between two posts that are eight feet apart. The dog is to the left of the handler in the heel position. Both the dog and handler are facing straight ahead, so that one post is at their left and the other is at their right. The dog and handler are prepared to walk in either direction.

When you start this exercise hold the lead in your right hand; your left hand should also be on the lead and should be about seven to nine inches from the choke collar. Of your two hands, the left one will be the more active.

PROCEDURE: To begin the exercise, call your dog's name and then give the command "heel." Step off with your left foot and turn to either the left or right. If you turn to the left, pass the first post so that you are in between the post and the dog. In other words, the dog will be on the outside. If you turn to the right, when you pass the first post the dog should be closer to the post then you are. In this case, you would say that the dog is on the inside.

Walk quickly and be careful not to slow down as you round the posts. Otherwise, if you change your pace as you come to a turn, your dog may get confused and think that you want him to stop and sit.

As you perform the exercise, constantly praise your dog by saying "good boy" or "good girl." With this encouragement, your dog will be anxious to please you and will do the exercise right.

PERFORMANCE: If you are doing the figure eight in class or competition, the exercise will begin with the instructor or judge asking if you are ready. If you answer "yes," this person will tell you that "you may go either way." This means that you have a choice of which post you will circle first.

As you are in the midst of the figure eight, the judge or the instructor will give you the command "halt." You will be expected to stop and the dog will be expected to sit in a good heel position. He must retain this position until you receive the command "forward." Then the two of you will resume the exercise and continue walking the figure eight until you are told to halt for the second and final time.

CORRECTIVE ACTION: There are three types of behavior to guard against in the performance of this exercise: Your dog may walk too close to you, he may stray on the turns, or he may stop "to visit" at the posts. These faults can be corrected by the following actions:

(1) If your dog is touching or crowding you, use your left leg or knee to push him away. As you do this, scold him by shouting the word "no."

(2) If your dog swings wide on the turns, speed up as you approach each post. Use several short jerks on the lead with your left hand to keep the dog close to your side.

(3) If your dog starts to sniff at the post, scold him by saying "no" and "shame." Pull him away from the post by using several short jerks on the lead with your left hand.

When you are satisfied with the way your dog is doing this exercise, you can prepare him to go off lead. To do this, place the loose end of the lead (which is normally in your right hand) over your right shoulder. The lead should be stretched across your chest and should still be held in your left hand. Continue the exercise and if your dog performs satisfactorily, remove your left hand from the leash. Keep this hand close to the leash, however, in the event that your dog needs correction.

While your dog is "loose," remain in contact with him by repeating the command "heel" and by giving him a generous amount of praise. This verbal communication will keep you in control even though you are not holding the leash.

Figure Eight

The two posts are eight feet apart. The dog must not brush them or sniff them as he makes his turns.

Using dogs as posts makes this exercise more challenging. This can be tried in practice but is never required in competition.

Imagine that you and your dog are separated and your dog is approached by another person. Will you be able to control your pet's behavior? Or will he become frightened and possibly snap or bite to protect himself? The Stand for Examination exercise will prepare you and your pet for this type of situation.

At the start of the exercise, your dog will be taught to remain in place when you give him the command "stay." He will learn to heed this command even when you are not at his side and you are not holding the leash. The applications of the word "stay" can be very important. For example, suppose that you are within shouting distance of your dog when a neighbor's child comes over to pet him. You can keep your dog from jumping on this youngster by simply using this command.

Later in the exercise, a person other than yourself will approach the dog and touch his head, back, and hindquarters. The dog will be expected to remain immobile during this examination. As he becomes accustomed to this contact, he will learn not to be shy or nervous when he is petted by strangers.

Not every dog will learn this exercise quickly. Some will sit when they are supposed to stand and some will follow their handlers when they are supposed to remain in place. If you have trouble getting your dog to stay, don't be discouraged. Refer to the section on corrective action and try the alternate procedures.

POSITION: Begin the exercise with the dog at your left and sitting in the heel position. Your right hand should be on the lead close to the choke collar. Your left hand should be free.

PROCEDURE: Pull the lead forward with your right hand and use your left hand to touch the dog between the right hind leg and the stomach. As you do this, start to give the commands "stand" and "stay." Repeat these commands several times until the dog is on his feet and perfectly still. Neither his feet nor his body should be moving.

When you are satisfied with your dog's standing position, place your left palm, with fingers pointing down, in front of his face and repeat the command "stay." (This instruction should be given in a firm tone of voice.) Start off with your right foot and walk counterclockwise around the dog. Make a complete circle so that when you are finished you return to the heel position. While you are doing this, remember to keep telling the dog to stand and stay.

If you are able to circle your dog three or four times without his moving, you are ready to proceed to the next part of the exercise. Walk away from your dog until the two of you are separated by the full length of the leash. Then turn and face your pet and wait for the examination.

In a formal setting (competition or class), the examination will be conducted by a judge or instructor. If you are practicing at home, you can ask either a family member or a friend to help. All this person has to do is approach the dog so that he or she is standing in front of the dog's face. Then the person should reach over, touch the dog's head, run his or her hand along the dog's back, and—finally—use one hand to touch the dog's hindquarters.

During the time that the dog is being handled, he must not move. If you notice that your pet is getting fidgety, repeat the command "stay." Once the examination is over, return to your dog using the technique you learned in the sit and stay exercise. If your dog has remained in place through the entire exercise, he is certainly worthy of your praise.

PERFORMANCE: In class or competition, the exercise begins when the instructor tells you to "stand your dog" and "leave when ready." Once you and your dog are successfully separated, the examination will commence. The instructor or judge will handle the dog in the manner described above and will then tell you to "return to your dog." At this time you will go back to the heeling position and you will remain in that position until you are told that the exercise is finished.

CORRECTIVE ACTION: Many dogs will not respond to the methods I have just described. If this is the case with your dog, do not hesitate to use the procedure that is outlined in Alternative 1.

Alternative 1. Once again the exercise should begin with the dog seated in the heel position. This time switch the loose end of the leash from your right hand to your left. While you are doing this, pivot 90° counterclockwise, so that you are facing the side of your dog.

The first step involves the loose end of the leash (the end that is not fastened to the choke collar). Wrap this part of the leash around your dog's stomach, so that you form a loop as close to the dog's rear legs as possible. Be sure that the overlapping part of the loop is on top of the dog and is held in your left hand.

Once the free end of the leash is circled around the dog's body, the balance of the leash will form a straight line from the loop to the choke collar. Grab this line with your right hand at a point that is close to the dog's neck. It is important that the palms of both hands be turned down. This will allow you to pull straight up on the leash.

By taking the steps I have just described, you will form a harness that will allow you to lift the dog into a standing position. When you do this, be sure to lift with both hands at the same time. If you want, you can also use the harness to move the dog to a different place.

Once you are satisfied with the way the dog is standing, take both parts of the leash in one hand and start to walk around the dog. As you do this, repeat the commands "stand" and "stay." If you are able to circle the dog two or three times without his moving, place the two parts of the leash on the dog's back. Continue in the same path and continue giving the commands. Assuming that your dog still does not move, start to widen the diameter of your circle until you and your dog are six feet apart. Turn and face your dog for a few seconds and then return to the heeling position. Redo the entire exercise. This time use the procedure that was described at the start of this section.

Alternative 2. The methods of Alternative 1 usually work. However, there are some dogs who still need extra help in learning this exercise. For these dogs, I have devised an original technique that has always been successful. This technique has allowed me to train dogs who would not stand or stay for anyone else. In most cases, I have been able to train these dogs in just a matter of minutes.

In Alternative 2—just as in Alternative 1—a loop is formed around the dog's stomach. This time, however, the overlapping part of the loop will not be held in the left hand. Instead, the loop should be tied in a firm knot. Avoid making the knot so tight that it will irritate the dog, but make sure the knot is secure so that it will not open in the midst of the exercise.

When the dog feels the loop tied around his body, he will think that he is still in the harness and that you are holding the leash. Because of this, you will be able to leave your dog and walk around him as you did with Alternative 1. As long as the dog is tied, he will remain in place.

When you have completed the exercise, return to the heeling position and untie the dog. Do the exercise again but this time keep the dog on lead. You will find that Alternative 2 is the most effective method of training a dog to stand for examination. However, the use of this method will be meaningless unless the dog is first exposed to Alternative 1. He must spend some time in the harness before you can expect him to respond properly to the loop tied around his stomach.

Fidgeting During Examination. Suppose that your dog performs the exercise well but appears to be nervous when he is approached by another person. You can prepare him for this part of the exercise by making the training more rigorous. When you practice at home arrange for your dog to be approached, touched, and circled by a group of two or three people. As your dog becomes accustomed to these people, he will learn to tolerate their actions. Once this occurs, it is unlikely that your dog will be ill at ease in the presence of a single examiner.

Stand for Examination

The handler poses the dog for the examination. When she is satisfied with his position, she will give him the command "stay" and leave his side.

The judge approaches the dog from the front, touches the dog's head, and runs his hand along the dog's back.

To teach your dog to stand still, you can form a harness by wrapping the loose end of the leash around the dog's stomach—as close to his hind legs as possible. A firm grip on the harness will keep your dog from moving.

If you knot the loop and let go of the lead, the dog will believe that he is still in the harness and will remain in place.

In the Sit and Stay section, you taught your dog to remain in place while you walked away from him. Once the two of you were separated by the full length of the leash, you concluded the exercise by returning to your dog's side.

In the Recall exercise, you will once again use the command "stay" and move away from your dog. But this time, instead of returning to your dog, you will train him to come to you. The command that is used to prompt this action consists of the dog's name and the word "come."

There are many applications of this command. For example, you can use the word "come" to call your dog for dinner. You can also use it to get your dog away from a troublesome situation. In either case, the word "come" should be prefaced by your dog's name.

POSITION: The exercise begins with the dog sitting at your left in the heel position. Your right hand is holding the leash and your left hand is free.

PROCEDURE: With your fingers pointing down, place your left palm in front of the dog's face so that you are blocking his line of vision. Keep this hand close to the dog, but be careful not to touch him. As you give this hand signal, utter the command "stay" and step off with your right foot. Move away from your dog until the two of you are separated by the full length of the leash. Then turn and face your dog.

At this point, you should be standing straight with your feet about ten inches apart. This separation will provide a space for the dog when you call him. Be careful not to pull the leash too tight; if you do, there is a chance that you will pull the dog off his sitting position.

Calling Your Dog. In this part of the exercise, the dog will leave his sitting position, walk up to your feet, and assume a straight sit in front of you. To get him to do this, you must first call his name and then give him the command "come." This verbal instruction should be reinforced by a firm jerk on the leash. By pulling the leash at the same time that you call the dog's name you are preparing him for the command that will follow.

As your dog starts to approach you, roll or fold the leash with both hands. By the time the dog is at your feet, the entire leash should be in your right hand and this hand should be close to the choke collar. Your left hand is free and may be used to help the dog

42

into the proper sitting position. If your dog is sitting correctly, there are four conditions that should be satisfied: (1) The dog should be directly in front of you. (2) The dog should be facing you. (3) The dog should be in a straight sit. And (4) the dog should be close to your feet but should not be touching them.

Finishing Your Dog. If you are in a class or competition, the instructor or judge will tell you to "finish your dog." If you are practicing alone, you can decide when to begin this part of the exercise. The first step that is required is to move the leash into your left hand and to hold this hand close to the choke collar. As this is done, you should call the dog's name and give the command "heel."

The next step is to move your left foot out to your left side and behind your right. When you do this, you will not be changing the direction in which you are facing. Your weight will automatically be placed on your rear foot. How far back you should step should be determined by the size of your dog. If you are working with a large dog, a good size step is needed.

To move the dog into the heel position, swing a slow arc with your left hand (the one holding the leash) and stop the motion of this hand when it is in line with your left foot. Then step forward so that your two feet are back together. At the same time move your left hand forward so it is at your side.

The dog will follow your left hand back to the rear position of your left foot. As you bring your hand and foot forward, the dog will turn and will arrive at your side. He will be expected to assume the heel position. While you are doing this part of the exercise, your right foot should never move.

If the dog needs help with his sitting position, you can straighten him with your free hand. Throughout the entire exercise, the dog should receive your encouragement and praise. You will find that this will motivate him to improve his performance.

PERFORMANCE: If you perform this exercise in a class or competition, you will receive three instructions from your teacher or judge. These are: "leave your dog," "call your dog," and "finish your dog." When you hear the first instruction, you should give your dog the command "stay." The second instruction should be followed by your dog's name and the command "come." When you hear the final instruction, you should tell your dog to "heel."

Some of the techniques described in this procedure are not standard parts of the exercise. They have been included to make the exercise easier for the dog to learn. However, once the dog becomes accustomed to the routine, the following techniques become unnecessary and should be eliminated.

(1) You shouldn't have to jerk the leash at the same time that you call your dog. With a little experience, your dog should learn to respond to your command without any other stimulus.

(2) When your dog approaches your feet, he is expected to sit. You will gradually have to stop using your free hand to help him do this. However, don't remove this assistance until you are satisfied with the way your dog is sitting. If your dog develops bad sitting habits, they may be hard to break.

(3) To finish your dog, I recommended that you take a step back with your left foot. This step is intended to help your dog as he moves from in front of your feet to the heel position. But, as your dog becomes accustomed to the exercise, you should gradually take shorter steps until you eliminate this device altogether.

CORRECTIVE ACTION: Do not begin your practice session until your dog is still. If he appears to be restless or fidgety, scold him in a loud voice by saying "no" or "shame." Do not give him the command "stay" until you are satisfied with his behavior.

If he does not respond to the first command, use the corrective action that was recommended in the "Sit and Stay" section. Then try to leave your dog again, walk to the full length of the leash, turn around and call your dog.

If your dog does not come when you call him and jerk the lead, get a firm hold on the leash and start to walk backwards. Take eight to ten steps to the rear and then come to a full stop. Pull the dog close to you and lift your right hand directly above his head. This will put pressure on the choke collar and will encourage the dog to sit. As soon as the dog's hindquarters touch the ground, lower your right hand to release the pressure. If necessary, use your left hand to adjust the position of the dog. To help the dog understand that this is what you want, be sure to praise him as soon as he is sitting. Repeat these actions several times until your dog automatically sits when you come to a stop.

If your dog is overeager, he may respond to your call by jumping on top of you or scratching you. To correct this behavior, wait for the dog to jump and then plant your knee squarely in his chest. Scold him by saying "no" and "shame."

Many dogs have difficulty finishing this exercise. They either fail to sit or they fail to walk around their handlers to the heel position. The best way to correct this is to practice. Isolate this part of the exercise and repeat it a few times at every session.

This is a difficult exercise that may require a lot of practice. While practice is an essential part of obedience training, it can also be overdone. If your sessions are too long or if you repeat an exercise too many times, your pet may become bored and lose his concentration. When this happens, his learning ability is likely to suffer.

To avoid boring your dog, try to have two or three short practice sessions during a day instead of one long one. Do not spend too much time on one exercise. Vary your program, but keep returning to the parts of an exercise that require extra work. To make your practice sessions more enjoyable for your pet, remember to praise him when he does something well.

Recall on Lead

When you call your dog, you should be standing straight with your feet about ten inches apart.

As your dog approaches, roll or fold the lead with both hands.

After your dog has responded to the command "come," he should be in a straight sit in front of your feet.

To finish your dog give the command "heel." As you do this, step back with your left foot and use the lead to guide the dog into the heel position.

Although we love our pets, there are times when they get in our way. Think of your own experiences. Have you ever had an important conversation interrupted because your dog kept wanting to be petted? Have you ever brought your dog inside only to have him constantly scratch the door and plead to go back out? Has your pet ever bothered you at mealtimes?

If you have suffered through these experiences, you have probably told your dog to "go lay down." The reasons for giving this command are obvious. You are not trying to punish your dog, but you do want him to leave you alone until your conversation is finished. Or you want him to stay away from the door until you are ready to take him out. Or you want him away from the table until supper is over. If you can get your dog to lie down, you can accomplish any one of these objectives. But if your dog hasn't been trained, it is not likely that he will understand you or obey your command.

In this section, I will show you four methods of getting your dog to lie down and remain down for an extended period of time. As you gain experience, you will be able to get your dog to lie down without giving him a command. All that you will need is the proper hand signal.

POSITION: The exercise begins with the dog in a straight sit next to your left foot. Once again—as with the other exercises in this chapter—the dog is on leash. The open end of the leash is held in your right hand.

PROCEDURE: There are many ways to train your dog to lay down and stay down. The method I recommend is the one that I have always taught in class. It has allowed over 95% of my beginning handlers to train their dogs to successfully complete this exercise. I will refer to this procedure as Method 1. If you decide not to use this method, you can choose as an alternative either Method 2 for small dogs or Method 3 or 4 for larger dogs.

Method 1. Leave your dog as you did in the "Sit and Stay" section. When you are separated from your pet by the full length of the leash, you should assume a new position by taking the following actions:

(1) You should turn so that your left hip is pointing toward the dog.

(2) You should hold the open end of the lead aloft in your right

hand, but the balance of the leash should be placed on the ground in a straight line between you and your dog.

(3) You should step on the lead so that it is underneath the arches of your feet. Keep your feet approximately eighteen inches apart. When you are in this stance, the dog cannot wrap the lead around your feet and pull you down.

In this position, you are ready to down your dog. To do this, give him the command "down" and approach him by taking small side steps. With each step, encourage your dog by saying "good dog, down."

Apply this method slowly and come as close to the dog's choke collar as you can. In almost all cases, your actions will cause the dog to gradually lower himself. Do not be satisfied with the dog's position until there is no light visible between his stomach and the ground.

Once the dog is down, count to fifteen or twenty and then gradually lift your left foot. Your dog may respond to the reduced pressure on the lead by trying to get up. If he does, return your left foot to its previous position and wait for a longer period of time.

Method 2. This technique can be used to train small dogs. As with Method 1, the procedure begins with the dog sitting at your left. But this time instead of leaving your dog you will kneel beside him. With your right hand, you will pull his front feet forward until the entire length of his front legs is resting on the ground.

At the same time that you move your dog's legs, place your left arm over his back and gently push or coax him down. As you lower your dog, gradually ease him onto his side because this is a comfortable position. Once your dog is down, count to fifteen or twenty and then slowly raise your left arm. If your dog considers this a signal to move, you should restrain him by returning your arm to his back. Keep him down for a longer interval before attempting to lift your arm again.

Repeat this action until you are confident that your dog will stay down without your assistance. While you are teaching him to retain this position, encourage your dog by giving him your praise.

Method 3. This technique can be used to train the larger breeds. Begin the procedure by getting your dog to sit in the heel position and by lowering yourself so that your knees are touching the ground.

Your right hand will be the one that is further away from the dog. Move this hand in front of the dog and grab his right front paw. With your left hand, reach over the dog and take hold of his left front paw. As you do this, your upper arm will bend until it fits snugly over the dog's shoulders. This part of your arm (and your armpit) will be used to put pressure on the dog and to lower him into the down position. Maintain the pressure on the dog's back until you are ready to test him. Then gradually lift your left arm and see if he will remain in place.

Method 4. You can down your dog using a variation of Method 3. To do this, kneel in front of your dog and face him. Grab a paw with each hand and pull forward until his legs are completely extended. When the dog's legs are straight out in front of him, he will have to be in the proper position.

Leaving and Returning to Your Dog. This exercise does not end when your dog lies down. As part of the routine, you must walk to the end of the leash and turn and face your dog for a period of three minutes. When this interval is over you will return to your dog by passing him with your left side, walking in a semicircle behind him, and finishing in the heel position. This procedure was described earlier in the chapter.

Many dogs will become excited when their handler returns and will break from their position before the exercise is over. If this occurred in front of a judge, the animal would be heavily penalized. To guard against early breaking, I suggest that in practice you make a habit of returning to your dog twice. Thus, when you arrive at his side for the first time, you will stay there for just a few seconds. This is effective because when you return to your dog in the future he will not be able to anticipate whether you are going to stay or leave. Because of this, he will not change his position until he has received your command.

Returning to your dog more than once is a device that is only used in practice; it is not a standard part of the exercise.

PERFORMANCE: If you perform this exercise in front of an instructor or judge, you will have to respond to five instructions. The first of these is "prepare your dog for the Long Down." This means that you should sit your dog in the heel position.

Once this is accomplished, you will be told to "down your dog" and you will be expected to do this with just a vocal command. In this situation, you would not resort to Methods 1 through 4.

After the dog is down, you will give him the command "stay" as you place your left palm in front of his face. You will take your first step with your right foot and walk to the end of your lead. At this point, you will turn around and face your dog. None of these actions should take place, however, until you have received the third instruction. This is "leave your dog for the Long Down."

Approximately three minutes will pass before you receive the instruction "return to your dog." When you are told to do this, walk back on the three o'clock side of your dog, circle behind him, and come to a halt when you and your dog are facing in the same direction and your dog is next to your left side.

Retain this position until the judge or instructor says "exercise finished." These words should be your cue to pat your dog and compliment him for a job well done.

CORRECTIVE ACTION: Method 1 is almost always successful. If, however, your dog does not respond as you approach his choke collar, you can use your left hand to gently push him down. When you do this, try to move him onto his side. Dogs generally prefer this position and if they are on their side they are more likely to stay for the full three minutes.

If your dog starts to move when you take your foot off the leash, do not hesitate to scold him by saying "no" and "shame" and place your foot back on the lead. Repeat this action as often as necessary until you are satisfied with his performance.

If you are unsuccessful in your attempt to use Methods 2, 3, or 4, I strongly urge you to try Method 1. This is a much more effective procedure and I have seen it work with over 2000 dogs. Despite this positive experience, there are some people who object to this method because they have seen dogs have an adverse reaction when the procedure is first applied.

If your dog is nervous or timid, he may start to bark or whine when you first step on the leash. If this happens, try not to get excited and don't stop what you are doing. If you proceed calmly and gently, this spell of nervousness will last for just a few minutes. At the end of that time, the dog will accept this procedure and will probably be trained.

Once your dog starts to respond to the word "down," it is a good idea to combine this command with a hand signal. At the same time that you tell your dog what to do, lift your right hand above your head with your palm facing the dog and your fingers pointing up. Do this a few times so that you dog will associate this signal with the verbal command. Then eliminate the command and just use the signal.

If you are successful, start to vary your procedure. On one occasion give the dog the command "down" and raise your right hand. On the next occasion only use the hand signal. Continue in this way until you are confident that the word "down" is unnecessary. Then eliminate the vocal command altogether. By doing this, you are preparing your dog for more advanced work in obedience training.

Downing the Dog

Method 1. To down your dog, place the leash on the ground and hold the loose end of it aloft in your right hand. Sidestep along the lead until the dog is forced into the proper position.

When you start to sidestep, keep the leash underneath the arches of your feet. Take medium-sized steps (rather than small) so you can maintain your balance.

Method 3. To get a large dog to lie down, you can kneel beside him, grab a paw in each hand, and put pressure on his back with your upper arm.

Method 4. To use this method, kneel in front of the dog, grab a paw in each hand, and pull forward until the dog's legs are completely extended.

CONCLUDING REMARKS

You have now read about the six beginning exercises. Before you continue to the next chapter, perform these exercises again and review your performance. Have you made any of the mistakes that are listed on the judge's worksheet on pages 56–57? If so, repeat the exercise and try to eliminate the flaws.

Another way to measure how much you have learned is to take Test 2 in the chapter on "Self-Evaluation." If you are able to answer almost all of the questions and if you can perform the exercises well, you are ready to progress to Novice work. On this level, you will start to take the dog off leash.

While it is good to progress quickly, it is a mistake to neglect the beginning exercises. If they are practiced, they will provide you with a strong foundation for your advanced work in obedience training. They will also have several applications in your everyday life. Perhaps you already feel that these exercises have made it easier to communicate with your dog and to control his behavior. If this is the case, your first venture in obedience training has been successful.

If there is not yet an apparent change in your dog or if he is slow to respond to your training, do not be discouraged. Many beginning handlers (including this author in his earlier days) have shared this experience. In my case, I stayed with obedience training because my instructor assured me that I would see a great improvement after the sixth lesson. Fortunately, my instructor was right.

When handlers become discouraged, their sense of frustration is somehow transmitted to their dogs. Because of this, the performance of their dogs will suffer. However, like other common problems in obedience training, this can be resolved through the use of corrective action.

What I recommend is that discouraged handlers go back to the beginning of the course and work their way through all the exercises. Usually, by the time the last exercise is completed, the handler is impressed with how much the dog has learned and the feeling of discouragement is gone. If this remedy is not successful, it may be advisable to stop training for a short period. During this interval, the handler should concentrate on playing with the dog and having a good time. When the practice sessions are resumed, the handler and the dog will have a better outlook and the results of the training will probably improve.

EXERCISE	NON QUALIFYING ZERO	QUALIFYING SUBSTANTIAL	QUALIFYING MINOR	Max. Points	Points Lost	NET SCORE
HEEL ON LEASH AND FIGURE 8	☐ Unmanageable ☐ Unqualified heeling	☐ Handler continually adapts pace to dog ☐ Constant tugging on leash or guiding	Heeling ☐ Fig. 8 ☐ Improper heel position Occasional tight leash Forging. ☐ Crowding handler. Lagging. ☐ Sniffing Extra command to heel. Heeling wide ☐ Turns ☐ Abouts No ch'ge of pace ☐ Fast ☐ Slow No sits ☐ Poor sits Lack of naturalness, smoothness Handler error	**40**		
STAND FOR EXAMINATION	☐ Sits before or during examination ☐ Growls or snaps	☐ Moves away before or during examination ☐ Shows shyness or resentment	Resistance to handler posing Extra command to stay Moving slightly during exam Moving after examination Sits as handler returns Lack of naturalness, smoothness Handler error	**30**		
RECALL	☐ Didn't come on first command or signal	☐ Extra command or signal to stay ☐ Moved from position ☐ Anticipated recall command ☐ Sat out of reach ☐ Leaving handler	Stood or lay down ☐ Touched handler Slow response ☐ Sat between feet No sit ☐ Poor sit No finish ☐ Poor finish Extra command to finish ☐ Lack of naturalness or smoothness ☐ ☐ Handler error	**30**		
	ZERO	MAX SUB-TOTAL		**100**		

LONG SIT (1 Minute)	Stood or lay down within 15 seconds ☐ Goes to another dog ☐	Stood or lay down within 15-30 seconds ☐ Repeated whines or barks ☐	☐ Forcing into position ☐ Minor move before handler returns ☐ Minor whine or bark ☐ Stood or lay down 30-60 seconds Stood or lay down after handler returns to heel position ☐	**30**
LONG DOWN (3 Minutes)	Sat or stood within 0-1 minute ☐ Goes to another dog ☐	Sat or stood within 1-2 minutes ☐ Repeated whines or barks ☐	☐ Forcing into position ☐ Minor move before handler returns ☐ Minor whine or bark ☐ Sat or stood within 2-3 minutes Sat or stood after handler returns to heel position ☐	**30**
			MAX. POINTS	**160**

☐ H. Disciplining ☐ Shows fear ☐ Fouling ring ☐ Leaving ring ☐ Disqualified ☐ Expelled ☐ Excused Less Penalty for Unusual Behavior

EXPLANATION OF PENALTY

TOTAL NET SCORE

Courtesy of Country Foods, Division of Agway, Inc.

3 The Novice Class in Obedience Training

This is the second course in formal obedience training. If you have successfully completed the work in Chapter 2, you might wonder if it is necessary to continue—or if your dog has already learned enough to make him an obedient pet. My own recommendation is that you keep on reading.

In Chapter 2 you learned many ways of communicating with your dog and controlling his behavior. These were important lessons, but they were based on the use of a leash. In actual practice, your dog spends most of his time with the leash off and these are the occasions when it is most important for him to be obedient.

To get your dog to respond to your commands while he is off lead, it is necessary to read this chapter and perform the exercises. When you do, you will find that much of this material is familiar. This is because the Novice Class uses the same exercises that were included in the course for beginners. The difference is that in novice work there are only a few occasions where you are permitted to use a leash.

HEEL ON LEASH AND FIGURE EIGHT

Before attempting the first exercise in the Novice Class, you and your dog should practice the many aspects of heeling. For example, you should work on fast, slow, and normal heeling; on left turns and right turns; and on the about turn and halt. Another step that you should take to prepare yourself is to review the score sheet at the end of this chapter. Pay special attention to the listing of faults for which a handler and a dog can be penalized. These are the things that you should watch for as you practice with your pet. Remember that although some of the exercises are unchanged from the Beginner's Course, it is now necessary to concentrate on the fine points. Should your work be evaluated, you will find that judges or instructors are more demanding in what they require from you and your dog.

In the Novice Class, the Heel and Figure Eight is performed on leash in the manner described in the second chapter. Thus, it is not necessary for me to give you much detail on how the exercise should be performed. Instead, I have stressed the ways that you can avoid the imperfections that would cause a loss of points in a class or competition. Even if you have no intention of showing your dog or taking him to school, it is worthwhile to try to eliminate these flaws. By doing so, you will gain the satisfaction that comes from a perfect or a near-perfect performance. You will also give your dog a better opportunity to learn everything that the exercise is supposed to teach.

In the Figure Eight, there are a few danger signs that let you know that correction is needed. Before I describe these, let me remind you of what the exercise entails. The Figure Eight requires two people to serve as posts. These people should be standing and facing one another at a distance of approximately eight feet. To start this exercise, you and your dog should be at a point that is midway between the two posts. If you are facing in the proper direction, one post should be at your left and the other at your right.

If you are participating in a class or competition, the person in charge will ask if you are ready. You should answer "yes" provided that your dog is at your left side and is sitting straight. Once you have indicated that you are ready to begin, you will be given the instruction "forward." At this time you should call your dog's name and then give the command "heel."

The Figure Eight is formed by your path around the two posts. If you round the left-hand post first, your dog will be on the inside between you and the post. If you start with the right-hand post, when you turn the corner the dog will be further from the post than you are. You must continue in the Figure Eight pattern until you receive the command "halt." This will be given twice—once in the middle of the exercise and once when the exercise is concluded.

The danger signs to look for are a tightness of the lead and a tendency on the dog's part to be distracted by the posts. A tight lead usually indicates that a dog is either lagging or forging. If lagging is the problem, you can correct it by giving several short snappy jerks with your left hand until the dog is back at your side. If your dog is forging ahead of you, you can correct him by pivoting on your left foot and bumping him with your right knee. A good rule to follow when you are walking the Figure Eight is to speed up around the post when the dog is on the outside and to slow down around the post when he is on the inside.

Both lagging and forging will cause deductions and both are faults that a handler should not ignore. One of the purposes of learning the Figure Eight is to eliminate this type of behavior.

Problems with posts range from a casual sniffing when the post is in the vicinity, to more severe problems where a dog will stop and visit instead of turning the corner. In either case, the dog is paying attention to the post and not his handler. While this is a serious flaw, it is not difficult to correct. Every time a dog becomes "involved" with a post, he should receive a sharp jerk on the leash and a good scolding. The words "no" and "shame" should be used to remind him of what he is supposed to be doing. If the handler is conscientious in correcting the dog *every* time he is distracted by a post, this bad habit will not persist for very long.

STAND FOR EXAMINATION
OFF LEAD

If you have read Chapter 2 and have taught this exercise to your dog, he is probably ready to perform it without a leash. To test him, remove the lead and give him the commands "stand" and "stay" in a firm voice. If your dog moves or if he is not sure of his part of the exercise, the corrective action is simple. Return to Chapter 2 and repeat the exercise on lead as it is described in that chapter. After a short practice session, your dog should understand what you want and should be ready to work without a leash. While success may come quickly, it is a good idea to rehearse this exercise on a daily basis until you are completely satisfied with your dog's performance.

The main defect to guard against is movement of your dog during the judge's examination. If you recall the procedure for this exercise, you will remember that the exercise begins when you stand your dog and give him the command "stay." Your next move is to leave your dog and to walk six feet in the direction that you and your dog are facing. When the two of you are separated by this distance, you should turn so that you are looking straight at your dog. At this point, you and your pet are ready for the judge's examination.

This begins when the judge approaches your dog from the front and walks right up to the dog's face. The judge will run his or her hand down the center of the dog's back and will then touch the dog's hindquarters. If the dog moves during this examination, he will be severely penalized. More important, if he continually makes this mistake, it will demonstrate that he is not learning what the exercise is supposed to teach.

To correct this, use the leash in practice and tie your dog in the harness I described in Chapter 2. Make sure that an examination by an outsider is part of your practice session. This will get your dog accustomed to the idea of being viewed and touched by another person.

Some dogs will falter in this part of the exercise because they are overly friendly. When they are examined by a judge they will either become playful or they will try to lick the examiner's hand. This behavior is inappropriate for the exercise and is sometimes undesirable in other situations. We all can think of times when a dog's uncontrolled friendliness has either bothered a visitor or has annoyed a passer-by on the street.

There is a simple method of correcting this behavior that can be applied in practice. To discourage hand-licking, the person who examines your dog should be wearing two white gloves. One should be moistened with water, sprinkled with pepper, and allowed to dry. The other glove should be saturated with white vinegar and should be worn on the hand that touches the dog.

After these gloves are used three or four times, a dog will lose his inclination to socialize with a judge. Most dogs, however, do not require this strong a corrective measure. Usually, if your dog starts to fraternize with an examiner, you can correct your pet by giving him a strong reprimand—the old "no" and "shame."

As you will recall, this exercise does not end when the examination is concluded. You, the handler, must remain in place until you receive the instruction "return to your dog." When you are told to do this, walk back on the three o'clock side of your dog, circle behind him, and stop when the dog is next to your left side and in the heel position.

You and your dog must then wait for the judge to say "exercise finished." Note that the interim between your return to the dog and the end of the exercise can sometimes be a troublespot. Your dog may be anxious to move as soon as you return to his side. It is important, however, that he remain in place until you give the final command.

The best way to train your dog to wait for this command is to return to his side *twice* every time you practice this exercise. What this means is that you will walk back to your dog's side, assume the heel position for a few seconds, and then leave your dog and return again. After you do this for a few practice sessions, your dog will learn not to move when you return to him the first time. Since you will only be returning once in a class or competition, you can be sure that he will remain at your side until the exercise is over.

While this corrective measure was suggested in Chapter 2, it may have to be applied again because your dog is now off lead—and being "free," there is more temptation to move.

A final observation is that taking your dog off the lead is much like watching your child swim in deep water. The first time you do it, you are likely to be apprehensive—but it is important that your nervousness does not show. If it does, your dog will sense your lack of confidence and will be difficult to control.

The best way to guard against this was described at the beginning of this section—practice the exercise with your dog on lead until you are sure he knows what to do. Then remove the lead and perform the exercise again.

If you have any doubts about procedure, please refer to the previous chapter. The description of the exercise in this chapter has been abbreviated to avoid unnecessary repetition.

HEELING OFF LEASH

If you have read this far without skipping any sections, you should be very familiar with the heeling exercise. You have already encountered it twice—once in the Beginner's Course and once in this course when it was combined with the Figure Eight.

Nothing has been added to the exercise. You and your dog will still have to make left turns, right turns, about turns, halts, and starts. But this time, you will do this without the assistance of the leash.

Before you make your first attempt at free heeling, it is a good idea to review the exercise with your dog on lead. This will give you a chance to refresh your dog's memory and it will also allow you to evaluate his performance. If your dog is making mistakes when he is on lead, you cannot expect him to perform better when the lead is removed. Thus, it is necessary for the handler to be patient and to eliminate all defects before attempting the novice version of this exercise.

The amount of time that you spend practicing with your dog on lead will be determined by the learning ability of your pet. As a general rule, two 3- to 5-minute practice sessions a day are recommended. Once these sessions are successful, you can start to think about letting your dog heel free.

The transition from on lead to off lead is not made all at once. It is a gradual process. The first step is to stretch the lead across your chest and to place it over your right shoulder. After you do this, let go with both hands and start to practice. Since you are not using the lead to control your dog, try to influence his behavior by your tone of voice. Praise your dog after almost every step by saying "good boy" or "good girl" and do this at regular intervals so that you form a cadence.

While you are offering encouragement, be conscious of the position of your left hand. It should be ready to grab the lead if your dog starts to lag or forge. When corrective action is necessary, the lead should be yanked with your left hand from a point that is nine to twelve inches from the choke collar. At the same time, the dog should be scolded with the words "no" and "shame."

As soon as the dog responds, the lead should be released and your tone of voice should be promptly changed. This method of training should be continued for a few days until the dog has demonstrated that he can accept his extra freedom and still do the exercise correctly.

When you are satisfied with your dog's performance, you are ready to take the next step toward your goal of heeling free. Drop the lead on the ground so that it will trail alongside of the dog. Practice the exercise and remain in contact with your dog by talking to him continuously. As you do, keep tapping the outside of your left thigh.

While you are no longer holding the lead, its presence still has an effect on your dog's behavior. This influence may be all that is necessary to keep your dog in line. However, if additional correction is needed, this can be accomplished by picking up the lead in both hands and by tugging hard. Once again, you may have to scold your dog by saying "no" and "shame."

Success in this training should be followed by still another step. Remove the lead quietly—so as not to distract your dog—and keep it loose in your right hand. Your pet should be able to see the lead so that he knows that it can still be used if his performance is bad.

When working on this exercise, keep your left hand away from the dog (especially from his head) or you may force him to heel wide. If it is still helpful, continue talking to the dog and patting your left thigh. Make sure that you practice all the aspects of heeling that you learned in the previous sections. If when you come to a halt, your dog sits incorrectly, you can use your left hand to modify his position.

The first few times that a dog is off lead there is a strong temptation to run away. To guard against this, it is a good idea to hold your first few practice sessions indoors or in an enclosed area. Possibilities are a garage, a basement, a courtyard, or a fenced in tennis court or baseball field.

If your dog *does* get away from you, do not make the mistake of running after him. Chasing your dog will make him think that you are playing and he will continue the "game" for a long time.

The best way to get him back is to start moving quickly in the opposite direction and to call his name and coax him to return. Once your dog is in range, put him back on leash and start heeling with the leash trailing on the ground. If while you are doing this your dog tries to get away, step firmly on the lead to prevent him from escaping. The sudden pressure from your foot on the lead will startle the dog and will probably discourage him from making further excursions.

After you step on the lead, you should reinforce the lesson by picking up the lead and jerking it sharply. At the same time you should scold the dog, so he is sure to understand that you are displeased. To conclude this corrective action, you should release the lead and try the exercise again.

Another way to prevent your dog from wandering is to keep small pieces of meat cupped in your left hand and to hold this hand close to your dog's nose and mouth. While you are heeling, encourage your dog in the usual manner and tease him by letting him sniff the meat. If your dog stays at your side, you should stop periodically and reward him with one of the pieces. This method has been used with some very difficult dogs and has almost always been successful.

After your dog has practiced heeling with the lead detached (but still visible in your right hand), you should try working with the lead completely out of sight. This is the way the exercise is performed in competition. It is the last step in the transition from heeling on lead to heeling free.

If during this transition, your dog has exhibited a chronic problem—such as forging, lagging, or heeling wide—you should attach the leash and perform the exercise as it was described in Chapter 2. This will give you a chance to correct your dog's bad habits and it may prevent both of you from becoming discouraged.

Once your dog is able to heel free, a good place to practice is a crowded shopping center. In these surroundings the dog will be so engrossed in trying to know the people who pass by that he will not have time to think about leaving your side. This experience will improve his ability to heel and will demonstrate the practical value of this exercise.

Preparation for Free Heeling

To prepare your dog for free heeling, stretch the lead across your chest and drape the loose end over your right shoulder. Let go with both hands and heel around the area.

The next step is to let your dog walk at your side with the lead trailing on the ground. If your dog tries to run away either step on the lead or pick it up.

When your dog first heels free, hold the lead in your right hand so your dog can see it. He will understand that the lead may still be used if his performance is bad.

In practice keep cadence for your dog by tapping your left thigh.

RECALL OFF LEASH

Many people consider this the most difficult exercise in the Novice Class. The best way to prepare for it is to review the description of the Recall in Chapter 2 and to practice this exercise on leash until you are satisfied with your dog's performance. Some hard work may be necessary, but it is important that you avoid overtraining your dog. Try not to rehearse this exercise for more than ten or fifteen minutes at a time. Remember that it is better to have two 15-minute practice sessions in a day than to work for a half hour, without interruption, on the same routine. The reason for this is that, without variety, dogs—just like humans—get bored. When a dog loses interest, his attention span grows short and he is not likely to respond to training.

Once you are successful in teaching your dog the Recall on leash, you should begin the following procedure to prepare him for the more advanced version of this exercise:

(1) Keeping your dog on leash, practice heeling.

(2) Without giving any signal or command, step out in front of your dog, turn so you are facing one another, and begin to walk backwards. You will be able to move in front of your pet, because he will slow down at the moment you turn into his path. If he doesn't, you can correct his behavior by bumping him gently with your right knee.

(3) Lifting the lead, but giving no verbal instruction, come to a full stop. When you are standing still, your dog should halt at your feet and should assume the correct sitting position. This response should have been learned from your earlier work on this exercise. If your dog does not sit or if his position needs improvement, you can use your free hand to correct him.

Correction may also be needed if an improper distance separates you and your dog. There should be no contact between the two of you, but your dog should be close enough for you to reach out and touch. If he is either too close or too far, do not try to move him by pulling on the leash. Any adjustments should be made with your free hand.

(4) Being satisfied with your dog's position, you can return to his side and continue heeling.

After your dog has mastered this routine, put the leash on the ground and repeat steps (1)–(4). By doing this, you are giving your dog some extra freedom, but you are still retaining the leash as a means of control. If corrective action is necessary, you can grab the leash near the choke collar or step on the leash with your left foot.

Since your dog can sense that the lead is still attached, he will probably behave the same way that he did when the lead was in your hand. If this is the case, you are ready to detach the lead. Try to remove it quietly without attracting your dog's attention. Stretch the lead out on the ground so it forms a straight line from your dog's feet to the place where he will finish the exercise. Then give your dog the command "stay," walk to the end of the lead, and make a complete about turn.

The next step is to call your dog and give him the command "come." He should walk parallel to the leash and sit in front of your feet, as he did in step (3). At this stage, your voice is your only means of control. Should your dog run past you, instead of using the leash to bring him back, you will have to scold him by saying "no" and "shame."

The procedures you have followed so far have been designed to eliminate the use of the lead. This is an important transition, but it is not everything that you have to accomplish. To do the Recall Exercise in the Novice Class, you must work without a lead *and* you must increase the separation between you and your dog. When you called your dog in the Beginner's Class, the two of you were only six feet apart. For the Novice Class, this distance will have to be increased to thirty feet.

The change from six feet to thirty feet must be accomplished in a series of gradual steps. You cannot expect your dog to adjust to this increased distance without a period of preparation. For this reason, I recommend the deliberate type of approach that you used when you were taking your dog off lead. The first step is to replace your six-foot lead with a lead that is thirty feet long. This new piece of equipment should be placed on the ground and should parallel the path that your dog will take when you give him the command "come."

The first time you work with the new lead, you should only unroll the first ten feet. This will be the distance between you and your dog when you make your about turn and call him. If your dog responds correctly, you can repeat the exercise and increase the length of the lead. This procedure should be continued until the entire lead is unraveled and your dog is heeding your command from a distance of thirty feet. When you have reached this goal, it is time to roll up the lead and put it out of sight. It may not be used in class or competition.

Without the assistance of the leash, you may have to give your dog some extra encouragement to obtain the proper response. Sometimes a few words of praise are sufficient. Other times you may have to tempt your dog with a fresh cooked piece of meat. This should be shown to him at the same time that you give the command "come."

If your dog does not perform well when the leash is completely removed, you should not hesitate to put the leash back on and to perform the exercise again. If necessary, the command "come" can be accompanied by a sharp jerk on the leash to remind your dog of what is expected.

The finish of the Recall Exercise is another place where many handlers have trouble. As you may remember from Chapter 2, the exercise is not over until your dog has been given the command "heel" and has moved from his sitting position to his place at your left side. When you are working with your dog on leash, you can teach him this part of the exercise by stepping back with your left foot and by swinging a slow arc to the rear with your left hand—the one that is holding the leash. Your dog will respond to these actions by following the leash until he is in line with your back foot. At this point you must move your left arm and left foot forward. This will cause your dog to turn around so that he is facing in the same direction you are. The movement of the leash will then guide the dog into the proper heel position.

The step to the rear should become unnecessary by the time you finish the Beginner's Course. Your dog should be able to move from one position to the other without any outside assistance. Only the command "heel" should be necessary. Where you are likely to encounter a problem in novice work is in the period that precedes the command. Your dog may anticipate the word "heel" and may leave his sitting position before he is supposed to. The best way to eliminate this tendency is to return to steps (2) and (3)—the ones where you moved out in front of your dog, walked backwards for a few paces, and then came to an abrupt stop. Your stops should now be followed by two different procedures. On one occasion, you should tell your dog to heel; on the next few occasions, you should wait for your dog to sit and should then continue to walk backwards. By varying your actions, you will prevent your dog from forming a pattern. He will have to wait for your instructions to know what he is supposed to do.

The important thing is not to lose patience and not to be discouraged. This is a difficult exercise and if your dog's progress is slow, you must be careful to hide your sense of disappointment. The best way to do this is to mix the Recall off lead with other exercises that your dog is better able to perform. By returning to these standbys, you can prevent your pet from becoming bored and you can rebuild your own confidence. By the time you are ready to attempt the Recall again, you and your dog should have a better outlook and should be more likely to succeed.

Recall off Lead

Your dog may have trouble adjusting to the increased distance of the Recall Exercise in the Novice Class. To help him, place a thirty foot lead on the ground and unroll it a little bit more each time you practice.

When you give the command "come," your dog will run parallel to the lead until he reaches your feet. This training device is never used in competition.

LONG SIT OFF LEAD

Every exercise has its own troublespots—places where you and your dog are likely to experience difficulty. In the Long Sit, the troublespot is easy to identify for anyone who has performed the exercise in a competition. The experienced handler will know that the difficulty is not in getting the dog to sit, but in getting him to remain still for sixty seconds while the two of you are separated by thirty feet.

At first you might think that this condition is nothing new for you and your dog. You have already been separated by this distance in the Recall exercise. What makes the Long Sit a little more difficult is that it is performed in the presence of other dogs. In some competitions as many as fifteen dogs and their handlers will perform this exercise at the same time.

What this can lead to is easy to visualize—dogs leaving their positions to sniff one another, dogs growling or fighting with one another, and, not uncommonly, dogs getting up and leaving the ring. All it takes is one dog to break the rules and it is very likely that most of the others will follow. While this is happening, the handlers are completely helpless. They are not permitted to leave their positions and they cannot call to their dogs to remain seated. Even if they could apply corrective action, it is very probable that this would not be forceful enough to counteract the attraction of the other dogs.

So what can a handler do to prevent the Long Sit from becoming a disaster! The precaution that is most appropriate is to get the dog accustomed to performing this exercise with other animals. If you enroll in a class, this will be accomplished for you. If you are training your dog by yourself, it is a good idea to have a few other pets around when you practice this exercise.

Of course, I'm getting ahead of myself, you can't practice an exercise or prepare for its troublespots until you have first learned how to do it. The learning of the Long Sit off lead parallels the learning of the other exercises in the Novice Class. The first step is to return to Chapter 2 and to review the exercise as it was described for beginners.

You may remember that the exercise begins with the dog in the heel position. The open end of the lead is held in the right hand; the part of the lead that is close to the choke collar is gripped lightly by the left hand. The loose grip allows the left hand to slide up and down the leash.

The first action is to give the command "stay" and to leave the dog's side. You should then walk counterclockwise and circle the dog slowly. As you do this, repeat the instructions "sit" and "stay," so that your dog will remain in place. If he begins to move, scold him by saying "no, no," and jerk the lead firmly with your left hand.

Each time you circle the dog, move a little bit further away from him until the two of you are separated by the full length of the leash. If your dog is still motionless, stop at a point where the two of you are facing each other and place the lead on the ground. Then walk back slowly to your dog's side.

Since the lead is still attached, the dog believes that you still have this as a means of control. Without removing the lead, give him a firm hand signal to stay and walk to the other end of the practice area. Then turn and face your dog and keep this position for sixty seconds.

After you have done this successfully a few times, gently remove the lead, place it behind the dog, and perform the exercise again. Practice three or four times a day until your dog consistently does this exercise well. As mentioned before, it is a good idea to include a few other dogs in some of your practice sessions.

There is no guarantee that your dog will progress from one stage to another without the need for corrective action. Whether the lead is on or off or whether it is trailing along the ground, the approach to corrective action should be the same. If your dog moves or lies down before the exercise is over, and does not respond to a brief scolding, the best course of action is to return to the heel position and begin again. If necessary, do this a few times until you are sure that your dog understands what is required.

Do not be too hasty in moving from one stage to another. Your dog may perform well on lead and still be a disappointment when the lead is removed. If this occurs, do not be too embarrassed to put the lead back on. Repeat the exercise a few times and then try it again with the lead removed.

Corrective action can be taken before a problem occurs. For example, precautions should be taken in advance so that a dog does not move before the exercise is over. The Long Sit is not concluded when the sixty seconds are up. The handler must still return to the dog and wait for a signal from the judge. To teach the dog not to leave ahead of time, it is a good idea to return to him twice—as I have described in previous sections. Returning to the dog and then leaving his side teaches him not to anticipate the end of the exercise. This device is used occasionally in practice, but is never permitted in competition.

The successful completion of the Long Sit in the obedience ring is a milestone in your dog's development. It shows that he can be trusted when he is off lead, away from his handler, and in the presence of other dogs.

THE LONG DOWN

This exercise differs from the Long Down in the Beginner's Course in two ways: (1) The exercise is now performed off lead. (2) There will be a greater distance between the handler and the dog.

The previous exercises in the Novice Class should have prepared you and your dog for these two differences. By this time you should be accustomed to working without a leash and the distance between you and your dog will be no different from what it was in the Recall or the Long Sit. Thus, you might use this exercise to prepare your dog for some more advanced work. For example, the hand signal for "down" is not required until the Utility Course; however, it is a good idea for your dog to learn this signal at the same time that he learns this exercise. For this reason the signal was presented in Chapter 2. As you may recall, when you want your dog to go down, you should raise your right hand so that your palm is higher than your head and your fingers are pointing up. Your palm, rather than the back of your hand, should be showing to the dog. Your arm should be close to your face but not touching it.

In the Beginner's Course, it was suggested that you use this signal to accompany the word "down." Now that you are more advanced, you may want to work on the elimination of the verbal command. To accomplish this, you should put your dog on lead and start in the heel position. Take one half step in front of your dog and turn so that you are facing him and so your hand will be visible. Then give him the double command—the hand signal and the word "down." Do this a few times until you are sure that the dog understands what you want. (If he is slow to respond, apply the method that is recommended in Chapter 2 for getting a dog to go down.)

After a few good responses to the double command, try giving the hand signal without the word "down" and see if your dog will react to just the lifting of your right hand. If he does, start to use the verbal command less frequently—perhaps two out of three times at the start—until it is eliminated altogether.

While you are learning to do without the word "down," you should also be shortening the hand signal. Your palm should only be above your head for a few seconds when you are starting to work on this exercise. As you become more proficient, the amount of time that your hand is in the air should be gradually reduced.

The teaching of the hand signal will help you with your later work in obedience training. Of more immediate importance is getting your dog to perform this exercise when you are not using the leash and when the two of you are thirty feet apart. To accomplish this, remove the leash and motion the dog into the down position. Start to circle him counterclockwise and, as you do, constantly give him the command "stay." If your dog remains in place as you walk around him three or four times, you can walk directly away from him until you are at least thirty feet from where he is lying. At this point, you should turn and face your dog and remain in position for approximately three minutes.

Since this is a long period, your dog may become fidgety and start to move. If he does, do not hesitate to scold him by saying "no" and "shame." If a scolding is not sufficient, it may be necessary for you to return to your dog and repeat the command "down" in a loud voice. When you do this, grab the ring on the choke collar and jerk it until the dog has settled into the correct position. Once he is lying down, you should give him the command "stay," walk away from him, and continue the exercise.

When the three minutes are over, or when the judge or instructor gives you the signal, you should return to your dog. If you imagine that he is at twelve o'clock and you are starting from six, you will pass him on the three o'clock side. When you do, circle behind him and stop when you are in the heel position. As with the Long Sit and Recall, it is a good idea to return to your dog twice during practice sessions. This means that you should only pause momentarily when you arrive at the heel position. It is recommended that you leave and stay away for ten or fifteen seconds before coming back for the second time.

The amount of time you spend practicing the Long Down should be determined by the learning ability of your dog. A suggested schedule calls for ten minutes of practice a day until the exercise is fully learned. Afterwards, it is a good idea to rehearse the Long Down three or four times a week so that your dog does not have a lapse of memory.

The three minutes that you spend watching your dog does not have to be wasted time. You can use this period to find out how your dog reacts to praise. While he is lying down in practice, offer him continuous encouragement and note his response. Some dogs will misbehave if they are overpraised. Other dogs need a steady stream of compliments to perform as they should.

CONCLUDING REMARKS

The Novice Course is the first level at which a dog can enter a formal competition and qualify for an AKC title. When a dog's performance is evaluated, the maximum score is 200 points. To obtain a passing grade, a dog must score a minimum of 170 and must receive at least half the points that are available in each category. For example, a dog who scores less than fifteen out of the thirty points that are awarded for the Long Sit automatically fails—regardless of his performance in the other exercises.

As you can see, a dog cannot make many mistakes and hope to qualify; near perfection is required. The same type of standards should be set by you, the handler, if you are training your dog at home. Do not move ahead to the next chapter, until your dog can perform all the exercises in Chapter 3 without showing any serious flaws. To get an idea of what type of errors to look for, please consult the judge's worksheet.

EXERCISE	NON QUALIFYING ZERO	QUALIFYING SUBSTANTIAL — MINOR	Maximum Points	Points Lost	NET SCORE
HEEL ON LEASH AND FIGURE 8	Unmanageable...... ☐ Handler continually adapts pace to dog. ☐ Unqualified heeling.. ☐ Constant tugging on leash or guiding... ☐	Heeling ☐☐☐☐☐ Fig. 8 ☐☐☐☐☐ Improper heel position...... ☐☐ Occasional tight leash. ☐ Forging. ☐ Crowding handler. ☐ Lagging. ☐ Sniffing...... ☐ Extra command to heel ☐ Heeling wide ☐ Turns ☐ Abouts ☐ No change of pace ☐ Fast ☐ Slow ☐ No sits ☐ Poor sits ☐ Lack of naturalness-smoothness ☐☐	**40**		
STAND FOR EXAMINATION	Sits before or during examination ☐ Moves away before or during examination.... ☐ Growls or snaps ☐ Shows shyness or resentment ☐	☐☐☐☐☐☐☐ Resistance to handler posing...... ☐ Extra command to stay...... ☐ Moving slightly during exam. ☐ Moving after examination. ☐ Sits as handler returns...... ☐ Lack of naturalness-smoothness...... ☐	**30**		
HEEL OFF LEASH	Unmanageable...... ☐ Handler continually adapts pace to dog...... ☐ Unqualified heeling... ☐ Leaving handler..... ☐	☐☐☐ Improper heel position...... ☐☐ Forging...☐ Crowding Handler... ☐ Lagging.... ☐ Sniffing ☐ Extra command to heel ☐ Heeling wide ☐ Turns ☐ Abouts ☐ No change of pace ☐ Fast ☐ Slow ☐ No sits..........Poor sits ☐☐ Lack of naturalness-smoothness...... ☐☐	**40**		
RECALL	Didn't come on first command or signal...... ☐ ☐ Extra command or signal to stay.... ☐ Moved from position. ☐ Anticipated recall command. ☐ Sat out of reach.. ☐ Leaving handler.... ☐	☐☐☐☐☐ ☐☐☐ Handler arms not at side ☐ Stood or lay down ☐ Touched handler ☐ Slow response ☐ Sat between feet ☐ No sit in front ☐ Poor sit ☐ No finish ☐ Poor finish ☐ Extra com. to finish ☐ Leaving handler. ☐ Lack of naturalness or smoothness ☐	**30**		
	ZERO	**MAX SUB-TOTAL**	**140**		

			Points
LONG SIT (1 Minute)	Did not remain in place . . . . ☐	Stood or lay down before handler returns . ☐	**30**
		Forcing into position ☐	
		Minor move before handler returns ☐	
	Goes to another dog . . . . ☐	Repeated whines or barks. . . . . ☐	
		Minor whine or bark ☐	
		Stood or lay down after handler returns to heel position. . . . . . ☐	
LONG DOWN (3 Minutes)	Did not remain in place . . . . ☐	Sat or stood before handler returns . . . ☐	**30**
		Forcing into position ☐	
		Minor move before handler returns ☐	
	Goes to another dog. . . . . ☐	Repeated whines or barks. . . . . ☐	
		Minor whine or bark ☐	
		Sat or stood after handler returns to heel position . . . ☐	

MAX. POINTS → **200**

Less Penalty for Unusual Behavior →

TOTAL NET SCORE →

EXPLANATION OF PENALTY

☐ H. Disciplining ☐ Shows fear ☐ Fouling ring ☐ Disqualified ☐ Expelled ☐ Excused

Courtesy of Ralston Purina Company

79

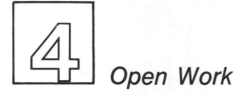

Open Work

You are now at the halfway mark in that you have completed two of the four courses in dog obedience. In the first course, your dog learned to respond to some basic commands. His understanding of these commands was more seriously tested in the Novice Course because most of the time he was working off lead and because the conditions for some of the exercises were made more difficult. For example, the separation between the handler and the dog was greatly increased for the Recall, the Long Sit, and the Long Down.

There are a number of reasons why the Open Class is even more challenging than the courses that preceded it:

(1) It includes more exercises. The Open Class has seven while the two previous courses had six.

(2) All of the exercises are performed off lead. In the Novice Class, the lead was used twice—for Heeling and for the Figure Eight.

(3) The exercises that are repeated from the Novice Class have been made more difficult. For example, the time limit has been extended for the Long Down and the Long Sit; and for both exercises the handler must be out of sight.

(4) Three new exercises are introduced. These are the Retrieve on Flat, the Retrieve over High Jump, and the Broad Jump. This will be the first time since the Beginner's Course that the dog will have to learn new routines. As you recall, the exercises in the last chapter were just advanced versions of the exercises you learned in Chapter 2.

Since each new course requires extra work, you may want to consider what you will gain from reading this chapter and practicing the exercises. Your dog—from his previous training—should already be more obedient and more intelligent than the average pet. However, there is still room for growth.

If you continue to develop your dog's abilities, you will find that he becomes an even better companion to you and your family. Furthermore, the new challenges of the Open Class will add variety to your practice sessions and will make them more interesting. This is important because practice is still necessary. While it is unlikely that your dog will forget what he has already learned, without the reinforcement of occasional practice he may become lazy and less responsive.

Thus, an argument for Open Work is that it may provide you with the incentive to keep your training program going. Another recommendation for this third course in dog obedience is that it can offer a new type of satisfaction. While you have probably been pleased to see your dog respond to the commands in the earlier chapters, you are likely to find the exercises in the Open Class even more rewarding. Most handlers enjoy seeing their dogs go over the jumps and enjoy playing with their dogs after they have learned how to retrieve. These are some of the accomplishments you can look forward to if you decide to read this fourth chapter.

Of course, any achievement that is worthwhile involves a fair amount of work. To be successful in the Open Class, handlers must be patient and must remain in close communication with their dogs. As in the previous courses, the handler's greatest ally is constant praise. To implement this, watch your dog carefully in practice. If he starts to do something right, don't be reluctant to show your enthusiasm.

HEEL FREE AND FIGURE EIGHT

Heeling and the Figure Eight are familiar exercises as they were included in the Beginner's and Novice Courses. What makes them different in Open Work is that they are both performed without the assistance of the leash. To prepare your dog for the removal of the lead, review these exercises as they were described in Chapter 2.

Walk through these exercises briskly with your dog on lead and make quick stops to keep your dog's attention. Watch for instances of improper heeling—forging, lagging or heeling wide. Most of these infractions can be corrected by jerking the lead with your left hand.

After about five minutes of review, remove the leash and continue doing the exercise. Observe the dog carefully. If he does not perform well when he is heeling free, don't hesitate to put the leash back on. One thing to avoid, however, is being fooled by a clever dog. At this stage, a dog can pretend to be sick or disinterested. If you oblige him by stopping training or by letting him do less than a proper exercise, this type of response may become a habit.

The best solution to this problem is to know what your dog can do and to expect him to do it. Don't feel that you are punishing him by trying to get him to do a good job. Be patient but also be firm. Demand your dog's best effort and when you get it reward him with your praise.

DROP ON RECALL

This exercise begins with the dog off lead and in the heel position. The handler will give the command "stay" and will walk straight ahead for thirty feet. If the exercise is being performed in a competition, the judge will tell the handler to call the dog and the handler will give the command "come."

This could be a description of the Recall Exercise in the Novice Course. What makes Open Work different is that the dog will receive a voice or hand signal for "down" while he is approaching the handler. This is a new experience for the dog. It is the first time that he has received a command of this nature while he was in motion.

After the dog has responded to the command by lying down, he will be told to come. The dog will rise, will walk toward the handler's feet, and will assume a straight sit in front of the handler. The dog will remain in this position until the handler gives the command "heel." In class or competition, this command is triggered by the instruction "finish your dog."

To prepare your dog for this exercise, you may want to repeat some of the procedures that were used in Chapter 3. The first step is to reacquaint your dog with the hand signal for down. Starting in the heel position, with the dog on leash, step out in front of the dog so he can see your hand. Then give the vocal command at the same time that you raise your right hand above the right side of your head.

If the dog fails to respond to this signal, repeat the word "down" and use the choke collar to jerk the dog into the down position. After it is clear that the dog understands what is wanted, I recommend that you use the verbal command less and less until it is eliminated com-

pletely. As you repeat this procedure, move further away from your dog until the two of you are six feet apart.

Success at this distance should be followed by the removal of the lead and an increase in the separation between the handler and the dog. The hand signal should now be given from a distance of ten to fifteen feet. After the dog lies down, the handler should walk back to his side and return to the heel position.

The next step should be to practice the command "come." Tell the dog to stay and walk straight ahead for fifteen feet; then turn and call your dog. If he does not respond, put him back on leash and jerk the lead at the same time that you give the command "come." Only do this until you are sure that the dog understands what you want.

Having worked on the two skills that are required for this exercise, you should now prepare for their combination. After the dog has responded to the command "come" and has settled at your feet, walk backwards for ten or fifteen feet and then call him again. As he starts to come toward you, give him the hand signal to go down. This may be a troublespot because many dogs will not comply with this request when they first learn the exercise.

If your dog halts when he is supposed to go down and then starts to creep forward, the following corrective action may be helpful. Walk quietly toward your dog, reach over, and tap him on the nose with the back of your hand. As you do this, give him the command "down" in a firm voice.

It is important not to scare the dog when you apply this measure. If you stamp toward him, move too quickly, or hit him too hard, he may shy away and put his tail between his legs. If this happens a few times, these responses will become habits and will be difficult to correct.

Many dogs will anticipate the hand signal or vocal command in this exercise and will lie down before they are supposed to. You can avoid this problem by varying your routine in practice. When your dog approaches you, sometimes motion him to lie down and other times let him come to your feet without interruption. By being inconsistent, you will prevent your dog from forming a pattern. Thus, instead of making a habit of lying down in the middle of his approach, he will keep walking until he receives your command.

As you continue to practice this exercise, keep moving further from your dog until you reach the desired distance of thirty feet. Pay attention to your dog's position when he stops in front of you. He

should be in a straight sit and should be close enough for you to reach. Any correction that is needed should be made in practice. The handler is not permitted to touch the dog when the exercise is performed in competition.

This exercise is important because it adds to your control over your dog. In performing the Drop on Recall, your dog has heeded your command while he was off leash, while the two of you were separated, and while he was moving from one place to another. It is worth noting that when you want to get your dog to do something in your everyday life, these are the conditions that normally exist.

Drop on Recall

As your dog walks toward you, you will give him a voice or hand signal for "down."

If your dog starts to creep, walk slowly toward him and tap him on the nose.

This exercise begins with the dog off lead and in the heel position. The handler will hold a wooden dumbbell in his or her right hand. After five to ten seconds, the handler will give the hand signal and vocal command "stay" and will throw the dumbbell approximately twenty feet in front of the dog. If this exercise is performed in a class or competition, the handler will receive the instruction "throw your dumbbell" from the person in charge.

About ten to fifteen seconds after the dumbbell is thrown, the handler will give the command "take it" or "fetch it" (either is acceptable) and the dog will go out alone and retrieve the dumbbell. When the dog returns, he will sit in front of his handler (as he did in the Recall) and will wait for the next command. This is the word "out." When the dog hears this word, he will release the dumbbell to the handler without offering any resistance and without letting the dumbbell touch the ground.

The exercise is not over when the handler regains possession of the dumbbell. The dog must retain his straight sit until he is told to heel. When he hears this command, the dog will return to his handler's side, as he did in the Recall Exercise.

In a class or competition, the actions of the handler will be prompted by instructions from the person in charge. For example, the command "take it" or "fetch it" is not given until the handler hears the instruction "retrieve the dumbbell." Similarly, the command "out" is not given until the handler has been told to "take the dumbbell from the dog." You have learned from previous chapters that most exercises end with the judge or instructor saying "finish your dog." This prompts the handler to give the final command of "heel."

This is the first exercise in which the dog not only learns to obey but he learns to provide a service. Since retrieving is a new experience for the handler and the dog, some extensive preparation will be necessary. This begins with the selection of the dumbbell.

The dumbbell should be made of light wood and should be wide enough so that the bells do not interfere with the dog's vision when he is carrying the dumbbell back to the handler. Before selecting a dumbbell, the owner should measure the distance between the outer edges of the dog's eyes and should make sure that this is less than the distance between the two bells.

Another factor to consider is the height of the rod (or "doll") that joins the two bells. If this is too low, the dog will have to put his nose on the ground to pick up the dumbbell. The dog will resent this and it will affect his performance.

Once the right dumbbell is chosen, the dog must learn to retrieve it and to keep it in his mouth for extended periods. These abilities must be developed gradually. You can begin by making retrieval a type of game.

While you are holding the dumbbell, roughhouse with the dog and occasionally throw the prop about ten to fifteen feet from where you are playing. Make sure that the dog can see where the dumbbell has landed and then urge him to go "fetch it" or "take it." To help the dog get the idea, alternate the use of the dumbbell with some of his favorite items—for example, you can throw a ball, a stick, or a marrow bone. When you do this, make sure that you give the proper command, so that the dog is learning at the same time that he is having fun.

In choosing objects to throw, avoid household items such as socks, slippers, or clothes. If the dog gets used to holding these items in his mouth, he may feel that you are condoning this behavior. As a result, he may revert to chewing and he may destroy valuable objects around the house.

Once the dog is accustomed to the dumbbell, introduce him to the exercise, but break it into segments so you can work on one part at a time. First, put the dog in the heel position, give him the command "stay," and throw the dumbbell. Wait for ten or fifteen seconds and then tell the dog to fetch it.

Many dogs will make the mistake of not waiting for the command; they will run after the dumbbell as soon as it is thrown. If your dog behaves this way, put him on leash and use the leash to hold him back until you give the command. You can either hold the leash in your left hand or place it under your left foot. Either way, you shouldn't let go until it is time for the dog to move.

Another, very different, problem that you may encounter is that your dog may not move when you tell him to fetch. If this occurs, put your dog on leash and when you give the command "fetch," walk him to the dumbbell. As you are walking, repeat the command.

If when you reach the dumbbell the dog makes no effort to pick it up, you will have to place it in his mouth. To do this, pick up the dumbbell in your left hand—the one that is holding the leash—and move your hand closer to the choke collar so that the dog is near your side. Put the thumb and forefinger of your right hand on the dog's lower lip behind the incisor teeth. Push down gently, to open the dog's mouth, and insert the dumbbell.

The next step is to teach the dog to hold onto the dumbbell. Keep your right hand under the dog's mouth to prevent him from dropping the dumbbell or spitting it out. Repeat the words "hold it" or "keep it" and heel the dog around the area. Stop every twenty feet and insist that the dog hold onto the dumbbell; then continue heeling.

Praise your dog while he is holding the dumbbell so he understands that this pleases you. When it is time for your dog to release the dumbbell, reinforce your praise with a small treat. If during practice, the dumbbell falls out of the dog's mouth, put it back using the technique described above.

When you are satisfied that the dog understands what you want, start to train him to take the dumbbell off the floor. To do this, put the dumbbell on a step or small chair and see if the dog will take the dumbbell without assistance. If he doesn't, attach the leash and hold it with your left hand close to the choke collar. Use this hand to apply pressure and jerk the lead. This will let the dog know that you are insisting that he take the dumbbell. It will also get him to open his mouth so, if necessary, you can place the dumbbell in it.

Once the dog is holding the dumbbell, praise him and count off fifteen or twenty seconds. Then give the command "out" and take the dumbbell away. When you do this, be gentle so that the dog isn't hurt.

After repeating this procedure a few times, take the dumbbell in your right hand and from a sit position heel the dog around the area. As you do this, hold the dumbbell an inch or two in front of the dog's mouth and tease him by moving the dumbbell back and forth. To give him the idea, keep saying "take it." (Note that while you are doing this the dog is still on leash.)

At the moment that the dog reaches for the dumbbell, you have two responsibilities—to praise him and to see that he takes it properly. If the dog does not get a firm grip on the dumbbell, you should use your left hand to change its position. Then continue walking with the dog and periodically remove the dumbbell and tease him again.

Before long the dog will progress to a point where he consistently reaches for the dumbbell and takes it from your hand. When this occurs, start to leave the dumbbell on the ground or floor. The dog will be expected to pick up the dumbbell and carry it around the area. If he does this properly a few times in a row, it may mean that he is ready to be taken off lead.

This is the last step before the dog practices the actual exercise. Once again the dumbbell should be left on the ground. If the dog picks it up as he did when the lead was attached, he should be allowed to walk through the Retrieve on Flat.

The first time this is tried, the handler should stay next to the dog through the entire routine. The dog should be well prepared for the fetching part of the exercise, but he will have to be taught how to bring the dumbbell back. This can be accomplished as follows: When the dog picks up the dumbbell, the handler will step out in front of him (so he or she is facing the dog) and will start to walk backwards. After a few steps, the handler will stop and will help the dog into a straight sit. The dog will be in front of the handler as he was in the Recall Exercise. The dumbbell will still be held firm in the dog's mouth.

After a slight pause, the handler will walk backwards again and will instruct the dog to follow. When they reach the place where the exercise started, they will both come to a full stop and the dog will sit in front of the handler. About fifteen seconds will pass and then the handler will reach for the dumbbell and give the command "out." The dog will be expected to release this object without offering any resistance.

It should be remembered that the exercise is not over when the handler gains possession of the dumbbell. It will still be necessary for the handler to finish the dog. This is done by giving the command "heel" about fifteen seconds after the dumbbell is released.

Some handlers will have trouble in walking their dogs through this exercise. If this is your experience, attach the lead and use it for corrective action. For example, the leash can help you heel the dog to the dumbbell and a few short jerks on the leash with your left hand can influence the dog to pick the dumbbell up.

The length of this explanation should demonstrate that this is harder than the average exercise. Therefore, it may require some extra practice and patience. However, if you approach the exercise one step at a time, you and your dog should be successful.

To get your dog to hold the dumbbell, put your thumb and forefinger behind his incisor teeth and lift his upper jaw. Insert the dumbbell with your other hand.

Once the dog has taken the dumbbell, prevent him from dropping it by placing your hand beneath his jaw.

Before your dog tries to pick up a dumbbell from the ground, let him try taking it from a chair.

When your dog has learned to pick up the dumbbell and hold it in his mouth, heel him around the area and keep the dumbbell in front of his face. As you do this, move the dumbbell back and forth and give the command "take it."

Walk through the exercise with your dog on lead. Then remove the lead, throw the dumbbell, and see if the dog will fetch it.

After the retrieval, the dog should sit in front of you and hold the dumbbell until you give the command "out."

RETRIEVE OVER HIGH JUMP

In the Retrieval on Flat, the dog learned to fetch a dumbbell and return it to the handler. This skill will also be required for the Retrieve Over High Jump. But in the latter exercise, the dog will be expected to clear a barrier on his way to the dumbbell and on his way back. The exercise is performed as follows:

(1) At the start of the exercise, the dog and the handler will be facing the high jump and will be separated from it by a minimum of eight feet. The dog will be seated in the heel position.

(2) If the exercise is performed in a class or competition, the person in charge will signal the handler to give the command "stay" and to throw the dumbbell. Ideally, the dumbbell should land about twelve to fifteen feet beyond the high jump and should be in line with the center of the jump. If the dumbbell lands too close to the jump, or if it is too far to the left or right, the handler will be permitted to throw it again.

(3) The dog must remain in place until the handler receives the instruction "send your dog." At this time, the dog will be commanded to "fetch it" or "take it." He will leave the handler's side, clear the high jump, and pick up the dumbbell in his mouth.

(4) Without pausing and without dropping the dumbbell, the dog will go back over the jump and will return to the handler. Once this has taken place, the dog will assume a straight sit in front of the handler and will hold the dumbbell until he receives the next command.

(5) This command—the word "out"—is prompted by the instruction "take the dumbbell." When the dog hears the word "out," he should give up the dumbbell without any resistance.

(6) The dog will *wait* for the command "heel" and will then move from in front of the handler to the heel position. The cue for this command is the instruction "finish your dog."

(7) The dog will remain in the heel position for about ten to fifteen seconds until it is announced that the exercise is finished.

During this exercise there are four pauses. The first occurs with the dog in the heel position waiting for the dumbbell to be thrown. The second occurs when the dumbbell is on the opposite side of the high jump and the dog is waiting for the command "fetch it." The third pause takes place when the dog has returned the dumbbell and is waiting for the handler to take it back. The final pause occurs when the dog is in the heel position and is waiting for the exercise to be finished. In a class or competition, the length of these intervals is determined by the instructor or judge. If you are working by yourself, you will have to establish your own schedule. A pause of ten to fifteen seconds before each command is recommended.

If you compare this routine with the Retrieval on Flat, you will note that the only differences occur in steps (3) and (4)—the ones that involve the high jump. Most people who read this description will have two immediate questions—"How is the height of the jump determined?" and "How does the dog learn to leap over the barrier?" Of the two questions, the first one is easier to answer.

The height of the jump is generally 1½ times the distance between the dog's withers (his shoulders) and the ground. For example, if this distance is eighteen inches, the dog will be required to clear a jump that is twenty seven inches high. Exceptions to this rule are made for the smallest and largest breeds. The minimum jump—regardless of the height of the dog—is eight inches and the maximum is thirty six inches. The rules governing the height of the jump can be found in the *A.K.C. Obedience Rules and Regulations Book.*

To teach your dog to clear the barrier, the first step is to obtain a complete set of jumps. You can purchase these or build them yourself. The jumps are not hard to construct and many handlers derive great satisfaction from producing their own equipment.

To start practice, set the jump at one-half the height that will be required for your dog in competition. Using the lead, walk quickly to the jump and hesitate as you approach it. Let your dog know what he is supposed to do by saying "hup" or "over" and by stepping over the jump with him. This won't be difficult even if you are not athletic. Remember that the maximum jump (for a large dog) in competition is thirty six inches. If you use half this height in practice, you will only have to step over an eighteen-inch obstacle.

After you have walked the dog over the jump a few times, he should understand what is wanted and you should be able to alter the routine. It will no longer be necessary for you to accompany the dog over the jump. Instead, when you reach the barrier, step to the side, and use the lead to guide the dog. Help him to go back and forth across the jump, and each time he prepares to leap give him the command "over" or "hup." In addition to these words, the dog should hear a constant patter of encouragement and praise.

To visualize this method of training, imagine that you have walked to the jump and at the last moment have moved to its right side. You are now facing the edge of the jump and the lead is in your right hand. Your body is stationary and only your right arm is moving as it follows the dog in each direction.

As your dog becomes familiar with this routine, you should change it in two ways: (1) You should give him the dumbbell to carry over the jump. (2) You should prepare for the dog's return by moving to the center of the jump. This way when he clears the barrier he will be moving toward you—just as he will be in the actual exercise.

Continued success in practice should encourage you to remove the lead. You will also have to raise the jump in installments until your dog can clear the height that is required in competition. Actually, it is a good idea to train your dog to jump one or two inches higher than the rule book would indicate. This will increase the strength in his legs and will reduce the likelihood of his grazing a jump when he performs in front of a judge.

Be careful not to raise a jump before your dog is ready. If you do, there is a chance that he may injure himself or become discouraged. When the latter happens, the dog will lose confidence and will shy away from a jump instead of trying to go over. The best way to remedy this is to backtrack. Put the dog back on leash and lower the jump. Work *slowly* until you progress to the point where the problem occurred. One of the secrets of successful dog training is knowing the pace at which your dog can move ahead.

Some dogs will be successful in jumping but will fail to pick up the dumbbell or finish the exercise correctly. If this is true of your dog, refer to the description of the Retrieve on Flat. In that section there are several recommendations for correcting these problems.

You may have the type of dog who will figure out an easy way of performing this exercise. Instead of jumping over the wall to fetch the dumbbell, your dog may run around it. If this happens, you can enlist the help of two people to stand at opposite ends of the jump. If your dog starts to run off course, these people will scold him and shoo him back to where he belongs. Usually, the presence of these people is enough to discourage the dog from taking the long way around.

An alternative solution is to work in a narrow area where there is no room for your dog to run around the jump. If this type of site is not available, you can improvise by placing the jump next to a house or fence. Either object will block off one side of the jump. The other side will have to be blocked by a person.

Throughout the jumping exercise remember to praise your dog each time he is successful. You may have to be patient and work with him for a long time before he will jump off lead and clear the required height. Once this is accomplished, however, you and your dog will experience a great satisfaction. Perhaps this exercise—when it is performed right—is more pleasing than any other to the dog and handler.

Retrieve over High Jump

The high jump should be 1½ times the distance between the ground and the dog's withers.

To start practice, set the jump at one half its required height. With your dog on lead, walk quickly to the jump, hesitate, and then step over it.

After you have walked the dog over the jump a few times, move to the side of the jump and use the lead to guide him over. Each time he prepares to leap, give him the command "over" or "hup."

When your dog learns to go over the high jump off lead, prepare for his return by moving to the center of the jump. This way when he clears the barrier he will be moving toward you—just as he will be in the actual exercise.

To prevent your dog from running around the wall to retrieve the dumbbell, you can have two people stand at opposite ends of the jump during practice.

The actual jump. If your dog grazes the wall in competition, he will be penalized.

BROAD JUMP

This exercise differs from the Retrieve Over High Jump in a few respects. Of course, the trajectory of the jump will be different—the dog will be striving for distance rather than height. Also, the dog will make only one jump, will not have to retrieve a dumbbell, and will finish the exercise in a different place from where he started.

If the Broad Jump is conducted in a class or competition, it will be performed as follows:

(1) The exercise will start with the dog seated in the heel position. The handler and dog will be facing the hurdles and will be a minimum of eight feet away from them.

(2) The first instruction from the person in charge will be "leave your dog." The handler will give the command "stay," will walk to the right side of the broad jump, and will turn so that he or she is facing the jump. At this point, a minimum of two feet should separate the handler from the jump. The handler may be positioned anywhere between the first and last hurdles.

(3) The next instruction will be "send your dog." The handler will respond by giving the command "over" and the dog must react by running straight to the jump and clearing it without grazing any of the hurdles.

(4) After the jump is completed, the handler will turn 90° to the right, so that he or she is facing in the direction in which the jump was made. The dog will do an about turn, will approach the handler, and will come to a sitting position in front of the handler's feet.

(5) The dog will remain in a straight sit until the person in charge says "finish your dog." At this time, the dog will receive the command "heel" and will move to the handler's side.

(6) The dog and handler will retain the heel position until they are told that the exercise is finished.

If you are performing the exercise outside of a class or competition, you will have to determine the intervals between steps (1) and (2), (2) and (3), (4) and (5), and (5) and (6). Gaps of approximately ten seconds are recommended.

A good way to start the discussion of the Broad Jump is to raise two questions that are similar to the questions that were posed in the previous section: "How is the length of the jump determined?" and "How can the dog be trained to perform the exercise?" Once again the first question requires the shorter answer.

The distance that the dog must jump is equal to twice the height that is expected of him in the High Jump. For example, if your dog measures eighteen inches from the ground to his withers, he will be expected to clear twenty seven inches in the High Jump and fifty four inches in the Broad Jump. As you may remember, the High Jump had minimum and maximum limitations. Regardless of size, the smallest dogs were expected to clear at least eight inches and the largest dogs were not expected to clear any more than thirty six inches. These limitations are doubled for the Broad Jump. Thus a sixteen-inch jump is the least that's required and a seventy two-inch jump is the maximum.

The first step in training your dog to do this exercise is to obtain the necessary equipment. This consists of four hurdles that have slanted tops and that vary slightly in their length and height. The shortest hurdle is 4½ feet long and has a low edge that is only four inches above the ground. The longest hurdle is five feet long and its high edge is six inches above the ground. According to AKC regulations, the color of the hurdles must be flat white.

When the Broad Jump is set up, the shortest hurdle should be in front and each successive hurdle should be longer. The number of hurdles to be used will depend on the length of the jump:

The two shortest hurdles will be used for jumps of sixteen to thirty one inches;

The three shortest hurdles will be used for jumps of thirty two to fifty one inches, and

All four hurdles will be used for jumps of fifty two to seventy two inches.

The distance between successive hurdles should be equal and each hurdle should have its high side at the rear.

Before your dog can go over the broad jump, you will need to give him some preliminary training. To start work on this exercise, take two hurdles and put one on top of the other. (Or, if you prefer, you can rest a board or hurdle on top of two stacks of blocks or boxes.)

Either way you will create an obstacle that will help your dog become accustomed to the idea of jumping. Close behind the obstacle you can place the remaining hurdles.

Once the obstacle is erected, put your dog on leash and walk him toward the jump. As you approach the jump, give the command "hup," jerk the lead slightly, and go over the obstacle with your dog. Then turn and go back to the place from which you started.

After your dog has cleared the obstacle five or six times, you can take it down and spread the hurdles to the distance that will be required in competition. Keep your dog on lead but alter the procedure as follows: With your dog in the heel position, give the command "stay" and walk to the right side of the broad jump. After pausing for a few seconds, give the command "hup" or "over." Your dog may respond in one of three ways: He may go over the jump as you directed, he may come to the jump and stop, or he may remain in place.

If he responds in the second manner, you can help him by picking up the lead and using it to guide him over the jump. When you do this, you will be facing the jump from the right side and will not be going over the hurdles with the dog. It is important to cue your dog by giving him the command "hup" or "over" and by tugging slightly on the lead. After you repeat this procedure a few times, your dog should understand what you want.

If your dog does not respond to the command "over" (that is, if he responds in the third manner), you should rebuild the obstacle and go over it with him again. The next step is to give the command "stay" and to move to the far side of the obstacle. Call your dog and coax him to jump over the obstacle and come to you. If he balks at doing this, get hold of the leash and tug it lightly to help him over. Praise your dog for clearing the jump and possibly reward him with a small treat.

Once the dog has learned how to clear the jump, he must be taught how to finish the exercise. To do this, stand on the right side of the jump and hold the leash as the dog goes over the hurdles. When the dog lands, turn 90° to the right so you are facing in the direction in which he jumped. Pull the lead to turn the dog around and bring him toward you. When he is in front of your feet, you can use your free hand to help him sit.

Once the dog has learned this routine, he has learned all the parts of the exercise. You may want to review the six-step description of the Broad Jump at the start of this section and then take your dog off lead and see how he performs. If you do, there are four common trouble-spots that you should be aware of:

(1) The dog may scrape or graze the hurdles when he jumps.

(2) The dog may jump across the hurdles at an angle instead of jumping straight.

(3) The dog may not return to you after jumping.

(4) The dog may not respond to the command "heel" at the end of the exercise.

All of these problems can be remedied. If your dog is scraping or grazing the jump, insert the obstacle between the first and second hurdles. Put the dog back on leash and help him over the jump. The presence of the obstacle will cause him to change his trajectory and get extra height and distance.

Handlers can use this technique *and* place their right foot in front of the last hurdle to prevent their dogs from jumping at an angle. This was the second problem mentioned above.

To correct the third problem (not returning after the jump), the handler can repeat the training that was used to teach this part of the exercise. Failing to heel (the fourth problem) is sometimes the result of the handler being close to the jump. If your dog exhibits this behavior, move further from the jump and see if he will respond to the command "heel." If he does, you can stand in this position for your next few practice sessions, and then *gradually* move back to the spot from which you started.

Broad Jump

To begin training, form an obstacle for your dog to go over.

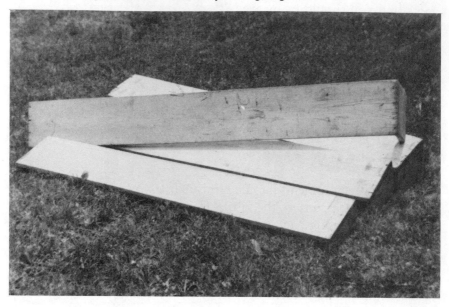

Start the exercise with the dog seated in the heel position. You should be facing the hurdles and at least eight feet away from them.

Give the command "stay" and walk to the right side of the jump. Position yourself between the first and last hurdles and turn so you are facing the jump.

When you give the command "over," your dog should run straight to the jump and clear it without grazing the hurdles.

After the jump turn 90° to the right. Your dog will also change directions and will come to a sitting position in front of your feet.

The exercise is concluded with your dog in the heel position. However, if you are too close to the jump, your dog may refuse to heel.

When this exercise was performed in the Novice Course, the handler left the dog's side and proceeded to the opposite end of the ring. The dog was expected to remain in place while in the presence of several other dogs. The proximity of the other animals and the distance between the handler and the dog made this a difficult challenge.

For the Open Course, this exercise will be made even more difficult in two respects. (1) The length of the sit will be increased to three minutes. (2) During this time, the handler will be required to be completely out of sight. From beginning to end, the exercise is performed as follows:

(1) The handler will sit the dog in the heel position and wait for the instruction "leave your dog."

(2) Upon receipt of this instruction, the handler will give the command "stay" in a firm voice and at the same time will apply the hand signal—the left palm should be placed a few inches in front of the dog's face; the fingers should be pointing down.

(3) The handler will walk directly away from the dog to the opposite side of the ring and will leave the ring for a designated area, which is completely out of the dog's sight.

(4) The handler will remain in this area until he or she is summoned by a judge or steward.

(5) All the handlers will return to the ring at the same time and form a straight line facing the dogs. The handlers and dogs will still be separated by the full length of the ring.

(6) The handlers will wait for the instruction "return to your dogs" and will then walk across the ring. During this time, the dogs must remain seated. They will keep this position even when the handlers have returned to their sides.

(7) The dogs will remain seated in the heel position until the person in charge announces that the exercise is finished.

If you are not enrolled in a class, the conditions of this exercise may be hard to duplicate. You will need to get other handlers and dogs to perform the exercise with you. You will also need to get someone to act as a judge and watch the dogs while you and the other handlers are out of sight. These complications should not discourage you from working on the Long Sit. Its practical applications are valuable enough to warrant the extra effort. However, if you are unable to get people to help you with this exercise, you should at least work with your dog so he develops the necessary skills.

The training for this exercise should begin with the repetition of the Long Sit as it was performed in the Novice Course. Once your dog demonstrates that he remembers what is expected, you should help him to get used to the idea of your being out of sight. This can be accomplished either indoors or out. In either setting, a great deal of patience will be required. This is because your dog may want to follow you the minute that you are out of sight.

If you are working with your dog indoors, get him to sit in one room of your house and give him the command "stay." Then leave the room and spend a short period of time in a different part of the house. When you return, you should immediately observe what has happened. If your dog is still in the same position, you should be generous with your praise; if, however, your dog has moved, you will have to apply corrective action. Scold your dog and sit him again, but this time arrange to have a means of watching him. For example, when you leave him you might go outside and look in through a window. If you do this, you should look at your dog from the side or the rear so he does not know that you are spying on him. The moment that your dog starts to move, he should be reprimanded with the words "no" and "shame." This may have to happen a few times before your dog realizes that you are in touch with him even when you cannot be seen.

For outside training the same device can be used. You can leave your dog sitting in the yard and quickly move into the house and observe him through the window. When you go inside be sure to use a door that your dog can't see, so he is not aware of what you are doing. Another possibility is to circle the house and to arrive at a spot that is a safe distance behind him. From this position you can watch the dog and scold him if he starts to move.

The amount of time that your dog is left unattended should be gradually increased until your dog can stay by himself for three minutes without violating your command. Once he can do this, you should give your dog a chance to perform the exercise with other dogs. At first, try the Long Sit with two dogs and two handlers. If you are successful (and extra help is available), the number of handlers and dogs should gradually be increased.

Your previous experience with obedience training should have helped you to develop control over your dog. The successful completion of this exercise should add a new dimension to that control. Now you can give a command and expect it to be obeyed when there are other dogs around and you are no longer in the vicinity.

THE LONG DOWN

This exercise was included in the two previous courses. In the Beginner's Class it was performed on leash and the handler and dog were never more than six feet apart. This distance was increased to thirty feet in the Novice Class, the leash was removed, and the exercise was performed in the presence of other dogs. Still further progress will be made in the Open Class. The length of the exercise will be extended from three to five minutes and during most of this time the handler will be out of sight.

The training for this exercise parallels the procedure that was suggested for the Long Sit. The best way to begin is to backtrack and make sure that your dog remembers what he learned in the earlier classes. Let him demonstrate that he can respond to the command "down" and hold his position without sitting, creeping, whining, or barking. Then, see if he can do as well when you are not in his presence.

To test him, practice in one room of your house and leave the room as soon as you have given the command "down." Return in a few seconds and see if there is any change in your dog's position. If he hasn't moved, he should be praised or rewarded and the experiment should be tried again. This time you should be out of the room for a longer period. If when you come back the dog is still motionless, you should repeat this procedure until you are able to leave your dog for the full five minutes.

Some dogs can be trained in this way, but others will try to follow you out the door or will start to move or bark as soon as you are gone. If you experience either of these problems, you will have to scold your dog and then apply the corrective action that was suggested for the Long Sit. To do this, you must find a place where you can observe your dog without being seen. In the last section it was suggested that this could be done by looking through a ground floor window. It can also be accomplished by using a large keyhole or by working in a room with two doorways. You would leave the room through one door and watch your dog through the other. The moment your dog violated the command "down," you would have to surprise him with a sharp reprimand.

For this action to be effective, your dog should not know where you are when you criticize him. Thus, if you have taken a roundabout route in getting to your observation point, you must be equally devious when returning to your dog. For example, if you leave your dog in the back yard and enter the house through a doorway that he can't see, you should use the same door when you go back to the yard. Keeping your dog curious is an important part of his training.

You may have to repeat the corrective action several times before you are satisfied with your dog's performance. Once he is meeting the requirements of the exercise, it is a good idea to let him try it in the presence of other dogs. If this experiment is successful, your dog has learned what the exercise is supposed to teach.

The practical value of the Long Down is easy to demonstrate. Suppose that you have the family pet and a few visitors in the same room. It is necessary for you to go to the kitchen to prepare some food and drinks. Now that your dog has learned this exercise, you can give him the command "down" and trust him to remain in place while you are out of the room.

CONCLUDING REMARKS

The exercises in the Open Class can be divided into three categories. (1) The Heel Free and Figure Eight, the Long Sit, and the Long Down are all more advanced versions of exercises that you have already learned. (2) The Drop on Recall requires a combination of two skills that were taught to your dog in the earlier courses. (3) The Retrieve on Flat, Retrieve Over High Jump, and the Broad Jump were all presented for the first time in this chapter. To appreciate the complexity of these exercises, you can probably think back to the many training sessions you spent with your dog. Another way to evaluate their difficulty is to refer to the judge's worksheet. You will see that your dog will have to exhibit several *different* skills in order to do these exercises correctly. For example, look at the requirements for the Retrieve Over High Jump. Your dog's performance of this exercise would be considered unsatisfactory:

(1) If he anticipated the command "fetch it" or failed to obey this command.

(2) If he refused to go over the jump on his way out or back.

(3) If he failed to retrieve the dumbbell.

(4) If he failed to return to the handler.

In addition to these infractions, your dog could be penalized for grazing a jump, dropping the dumbbell, sitting improperly, giving up the dumbbell improperly, or failing to finish the exercise in a good heel position.

The point is that the requirements of this exercise are far more varied than the requirements of the exercises in the previous courses. Because of this, there is a greater likelihood of error. While you are learning an exercise, you can refer to the judge's worksheet to see the type of mistakes that you will have to avoid. Once you have completed this course, you may want to look back to the worksheet to appreciate how much you have accomplished.

EXERCISE	NON QUALIFYING ZERO	QUALIFYING SUBSTANTIAL	MINOR	Maximum Points	Points Off	NET SCORE
HEEL FREE AND FIGURE 8	Unmanageable . . . ☐ Unqualified heeling ☐ Handler continually adapts pace to dog ☐	☐ . . Improper heel position . . . . ☐ ☐ Forging . . . . ☐ Crowding handler . ☐ ☐ Lagging . . . . ☐ Sniffing . . ☐ ☐ . . . Extra command to heel . . . . ☐ ☐ Heeling wide ☐ on turns ☐ abouts ☐ No change of pace ☐ fast ☐ slow ☐ . . . . No sit . . . Poor sits . ☐ ☐ . Lacks naturalness smoothness . ☐	Heeling Fig. 8 ☐☐ ☐☐ ☐☐	**40**		
DROP ON RECALL	Extra com. or sig. to stay after handler leaves . . . ☐ Moved from place left . . . . ☐ Anticipated: Recall . . . . ☐ Drop . . . . ☐ Come in . . . . . . ☐ Sat out of reach . . ☐ Does not come on first command or signal . . . . ☐ Does not drop on first command or signal . . . . ☐	☐ Stood or lay down Touching handler ☐ Extra com. or sig. Sat between feet ☐ Before leaving ☐ Finish Poor sit ☐ Slow response Poor finish . . . ☐ Slow return Lack of naturalness ☐ Slow drop smoothness . . . ☐ No sit in front ☐ No finish	☐☐☐☐ ☐	**30**		
RETRIEVE ON FLAT	Fails to go out on first command or signal . . . ☐ Extra command or signal . . . . ☐ Fails to retrieve . . ☐ Sat out of reach . . ☐	☐ . Slow . . . . ☐ Going . . . ☐ Returning . ☐ . . . . Mouthing or Playing . . . ☐ ☐ Dropping dumbbell Touching handler ☐ Poor delivery Sat between feet ☐ No sit in front Poor sit . . . ☐ No finish Poor finish . ☐ Handler error	☐☐☐☐☐ ☐	**20**		

Exercise			Points
RETRIEVE OVER HIGH JUMP	Fails to go out on first command or signal ☐ Fails to jump going or returning ☐ Fails to retrieve ☐	Goes before command or signal ☐ Jumps only one direction ☐ Sat out of reach ☐ Extra command or signal ☐ Climbing jump ☐	Slow ☐ . . Going ☐ . . . ☐ Returning . . . . . . Mouthing or Playing ☐ Dropping dumbbell ☐ Touching handler ☐ Poor delivery ☐ Sat between feet ☐ Touching jump ☐ Poor sit ☐ No sit in front ☐ Poor finish ☐ No finish ☐ Handler error ☐	**30**
BROAD JUMP	Refuses to jump on first command or signal ☐ Walks over any part ☐	Goes before command or signal ☐ Does not clear jump ☐ Sat out of reach ☐	Minor jump touch ☐ Touching handler ☐ Poor return ☐ Sat between feet ☐ No sit in front ☐ Poor sit ☐ No finish ☐ Poor finish ☐	**20**
	ZERO		**MAX. SUB-TOTAL ↑**	**140**
LONG SIT (3 Minutes)	Did not remain in place ☐ Goes to another dog ☐	Stood or lay down before handler returns ☐ Repeated whines or barks ☐	Minor move after handler returns ☐ Minor move before handler returns to heel position ☐ ☐ Minor whine or bark ☐ Handler error ☐	**30**
LONG DOWN (5 Minutes)	Did not remain in place ☐ Goes to another dog ☐	Stood or sat before handler returns ☐ Repeated whines or barks ☐	Minor move after handler returns ☐ Minor move before handler returns to heel position ☐ ☐ Minor whine or bark ☐ Handler error ☐	**30**
			MAXIMUM POINTS ↑	**200**
			Less Penalty for Unusual Behavior ↑	

☐ H. Disciplining ☐ Shows fear ☐ Fouling ring ☐ Disqualified ☐ Expelled ☐ Excused

TOTAL NET SCORE ↑

Courtesy of Ralston Purina Company

The Utility Course

Throughout Chapters 1–4 you have been constantly advised of the importance of praising your dog. Perhaps at times these reminders have seemed repetitious; they were only included because praise is an essential part of obedience training.

At this point, the author would like to pause for a moment and offer praise to you, the reader. If you have successfully completed the first four chapters, you have already trained your dog to be more responsive and more intelligent than the overwhelming majority of dogs in your community. This superiority should be apparent not only in the obedience ring but in your dog's everyday behavior. What is important to point out (although it should be obvious) is that your dog's accomplishments would not have been possible without you.

To take your dog from the beginner's level to the end of the Open Course required patience and hard work. Perhaps your greatest contribution to your dog's success was your determination to continue his training—even when his progress was slow and it was easy to become discouraged. As a result of your persistence, your dog should now be able to learn almost anything that you are willing to teach. The Utility Course will present him with a challenge, but he should be equal to the task.

It is recommended that you work on the exercises in this course to complete your dog's education. You will find that Utility Work differs from the previous courses in that there is a greater use of hand signals and there is more separation between the handler and the dog. Most of the Utility exercises do not resemble the work that you have done in the past. The one exception is the Signal Exercise in which the dog will perform such familiar actions as dropping, sitting, or coming to the handler. All of these actions will be prompted by gestures rather than verbal commands. The teaching of this exercise will follow the discussion of Scent Discrimination. The latter exercise is generally considered the most difficult and the most important in this course.

SCENT DISCRIMINATION

If you review the outline of this exercise, you will notice that much of the material is familiar. For example, in Scent Discrimination you will tell your dog to "find it" when you want him to retrieve an object; you will give the command "out" when you want the object to be released into your hands; and, finally, you will use the command "heel" when it is time to finish your dog. All of these activities and two of the three commands were a part of the Retrieve on Flat. However, that exercise was much simpler than Scent Discrimination because of a few important differences.

In the Retrieve on Flat you worked with one item (a dumbbell) that your dog could easily locate because he watched it being thrown. This is not the case with Scent Discrimination, where nine articles are used instead of one. Eight are left in a retrieval area and the ninth (the object to be found) is placed with the others after the dog is facing in the opposite direction. Thus, unlike the Retrieve on Flat, your dog does not know the whereabouts of the item to be retrieved. To find the article and to distinguish it from all others, the dog must rely on his sense of smell. From start to finish, the exercise is performed as follows:

(1) Before the exercise begins, the judge (or person in charge) will examine your equipment. You will need to have two sets of articles. Each set must contain five identical objects that are clearly numbered and that are not more than six inches in length. If you want, you can select objects that your dog would encounter in his everyday life.

One set of articles must be made of rigid metal. The other set must be made of leather and must have nothing but leather visible, with the exception of a few strands of material or metal that are needed to keep the article intact.

(2) The person in charge will select one article from each set. These articles will be placed on a table or chair that is close to the starting point.

(3) The eight remaining articles will be scattered in an area that is roughly fifteen feet in front of you and your dog. The separation between items in this area will be about six inches. While the items are being distributed, the dog will be sitting in the heel position.

(4) You will be instructed to make an about turn with your dog, so that the two of you are facing away from the retrieval area. The person

in charge will then ask you to select one of the items on the table or chair. You will be allowed to put your scent on this item by rubbing it vigorously with both hands. When you do this, be sure to cover the entire surface and work especially hard on the two ends.

(5) When you are asked to give the article to the person in charge, place the article on the clipboard or worksheet that this person is carrying. The clipboard or worksheet will then be used to transport the item to the retrieval area. It is important that this article be kept away from any other person's hands. Otherwise, someone else's scent will be mixed with your own.

(6) When you are told to send your dog, there are three things that you should do: (a) Cup your left hand over the dog's nose so he becomes familiar with your scent; (b) make an about turn so that you and your dog are facing the retrieval area; (c) give your dog the command "find it" so he will retrieve the article.

(7) Following your command, your dog should move briskly to the retrieval area and should sniff each article until he finds the right one. He will be given a reasonable amount of time to make his selection. Once he has picked up the proper article, he should return quickly to you and sit in front of your feet.

(8) The dog should keep the article in his mouth until you receive the instruction "take it." At this time you will give the command "out" and will reach for the article. The dog will be expected to relinquish it without hesitation or resistance.

(9) When you are told to finish your dog you will give the command "heel." Your dog will move from in front of your feet to his customary position at your left side.

You will note that steps (1)-(5) are merely preparation for the performance of the exercise and steps (8) and (9) are a repetition of procedures that you learned in the last chapter. Thus, your training program should concentrate on the activities that take place in steps (6) and (7)—the steps where you send your dog to the retrieval area and he searches for the proper item.

To introduce your dog to this part of the exercise, it is suggested that you practice with a set of five wooden articles in addition to the metal and leather articles that are required by the AKC. The purpose of including the extra items is to increase your dog's discriminatory power and to make it easier for him to do this exercise when only two types of material are being used. In this sense, practicing with the extra items is like a baseball player warming up with an extra bat.

Another reason for practicing with wooden articles is that it prepares your dog to accept other items. This trait is important if you want your dog to qualify for the tracking program that is described in the AKC rule book.

The third set of articles was once a standard part of the equipment for this exercise. The rule book in the United States has since been altered, but when the author last competed in Bermuda and Canada the extra set was still being used.

When you have selected equipment for this exercise, you should verify that your dog will retrieve each type of material. This can be accomplished by throwing an article a few feet in front of your dog and by instructing him to fetch it. If the dog picks up the article without hesitation, you are ready to continue.

The next step in your training program might be the construction of a practice square. This can be made from a sheet of plywood that is three feet on all sides. The practice square should have three rows of equally spaced 1/8" holes. Each row should contain four holes and each of the holes should be used to secure an article. The articles can be tied to the board with insulated wire or with pieces of strong string. If the articles are tied tightly, it will prevent the dog from picking up an object that he is supposed to leave alone.

Some dogs may resist this type of training because they dislike the wooden surface. If your dog does not want to work with the wooden board, try to create the same type of device by cutting a square patch out of an old carpet. Punch holes in the carpet and use these holes to fasten the articles to the surface.

When either of these devices is ready, place it on the ground and put your dog on leash. Escort him to a spot where he will be *sitting* and looking at the practice board from a distance of five to eight feet. Then, when your dog is settled, leave his side and position the scented object. For your first trial, this should be placed about three to four feet from the other articles.

To begin practice, you will return to the heel position, give your dog the scent of your left hand and then give him the command "find it." As your dog learns the exercise, he will respond to this command by going off on his own and coming back with the right object. At this stage, however, it will be necessary for you to walk with your dog and steer him in the right direction. As you approach the area that contains the scented article, you should encourage your dog to pick it up.

Repeat this procedure four or five times and each time move the scented object closer to the other articles. If your dog continues to perform as he should, your next step will be to place the scented object on the practice square.

When this is done, return to your dog's side, give him the command, and lead him to the practice square. Once you have reached this area, pay special attention to your dog's behavior. If he seems bewildered, point to the object that you want him to pick up. This will help him to understand that he is supposed to make a selection.

If your dog tries to retrieve an unscented article, he will be discouraged in two ways: (1) He will be unable to lift it off the practice square, and (2) he will be rebuked by you, the handler. A few failures will give your dog the incentive to sniff out the right article. When he has done this successfully four times in a row, he will be ready to try the exercise without the leash.

This is another example of the gradual approach to obedience training. You will notice that in the method just described your dog's progress was made in small steps. First, the scented article was moved closer to the others; then your dog had to perform the exercise several times before he was allowed to try it without a leash. While this approach requires patience, it is sometimes faster than trying to take a shortcut. When you eliminate steps, you make the learning process harder and there is a better chance that the handler and the dog will become discouraged.

You can, however, save yourself some work by teaching this exercise without the practice square. To do this, take five articles of the same material and scatter four of them on the ground. Your dog may be watching from the starting place while these articles are positioned. But when you are ready to place the fifth article your dog should be turned around. This article should be rubbed vigorously—so it is covered with your scent—and should be placed on the outside (rather than in the center) of the group.

To begin training, your dog should be on leash and in the heel position. The two of you should be standing eight to ten feet from the retrieval area and should be facing in the opposite direction. The first step is to cup your hand in front of the dog's nose so he can become familiar with your scent. The second step is to make an about turn and to give the command "find it." Following this instruction, you will walk toward the scented article and point in its direction.

If your dog takes your cue and approaches this article, you should encourage him by saying "take it." If, however, he wanders over to the other articles, you can allow him to sniff them but do not permit him to pick them up. The moment he tries to take one in his mouth, scold him by saying "no" and gently guide him to the proper object. When this article is taken, praise your dog lavishly so that he knows he has done the right thing. Then walk backwards with your dog until you reach the starting point and have him hold and then release the article as he would in the actual exercise.

When you have completed this routine, there will still be four articles on the ground. Leave these where they are and put the scented article in a new position. In deciding where to place it, you should consider the following three rules:

(1) The article should be kept on the outside of the group so it is still easy to find.

(2) The distance between the scented and unscented articles should be decreased.

(3) The scented article should be placed in a different part of the retrieval area.

The purpose of rule (3) is to prevent your dog from looking in the same location every time. If the scented article is always to the left or to the right of the group, your dog will start to depend on his sense of direction rather than his sense of smell.

The pattern of advancement with this technique is the same as with the practice square. The scented article is moved closer and closer to the group until finally it is placed in the center. When this is done, the dog should perform the exercise successfully at least four times before he is allowed to try it without a leash.

Success with this technique is not automatic. Some dogs will experience difficulty when the article is in the center of the group or when they have to perform the exercise without the lead. If this happens with your dog, the remedy is to backtrack. Think back to the conditions when he made his last successful retrieval. If you were using the lead, put it back on; if the scented article was on the outside of the group, move it back to its previous position.

When your dog has learned the exercise with objects of one type of material, try him with the other type, and then mix both types together. When both leather and metal objects are used, the number of unscented items will be increased from four to eight. The handling of these items is very important.

They should not be touched by someone other than yourself or there will be a mixture of scents that your dog will find confusing. It is also necessary to remove your own scent by washing these articles frequently with soap and water. After each washing, the article should be allowed to dry in the sun for eight to ten hours. When there is not sufficient time for this long a drying period, it can be reduced by at least half if the articles are washed in alcohol.

Some handlers may be interested in preparing their dogs for tracking. These people will need to practice the exercise daily and will want to introduce a different type of material in every session.

Scent Discrimination

The practice square. This training device contains three rows of equally spaced holes. Each row contains four holes and each hole is used to secure an article. The articles can be tied to the board with insulated wire or with pieces of strong string.

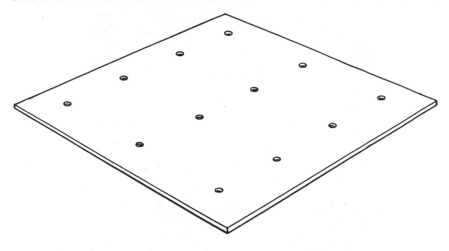

Instead of using the practice square, you can get your dog accustomed to finding the scented article in different places within the retrieval area. Dumbbell 1 represents the position of the scented article the first time Scent Discrimination is practiced. Dumbbell 2 shows the location of this article on the second trial, etc.

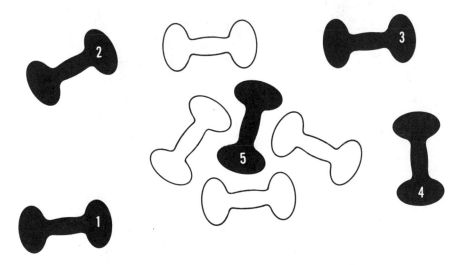

Leather and metal objects scattered in an area that is about fifteen feet from the dog and handler. The items should be approximately six inches apart.

The person in charge will select one metal and one leather object. These will be placed on a table or chair that is close to the starting point.

When you are asked to give the scented article to the person in charge, place the article on the clipboard or worksheet that this person is carrying.

When you are told to send your dog, cup your left hand over the dog's nose so he becomes familiar with your scent.

THE SIGNAL EXERCISE

From the previous courses in obedience training, you and your dog have developed a common language. Your dog has learned to understand you when you use words such as "stay," "down," "sit," or "come." At the same time, he has learned to respond to these words in a predictable manner.

In this exercise you will be looking for the same responses but your means of communication will be different. In place of verbal commands you will give your dog hand signals. Your dog will be expected to react to these signals in the same way that he responded to your spoken instructions. The exercise is performed as follows:

(1) With your dog off lead, heel around the area.

(2) Give the hand signal for "stay," so that your dog stops walking and remains stationary in a standing position.

(3) Repeat the hand signal for "stay" and leave your dog for the other side of the ring or area. When you have reached your destination, turn and face your dog.

(4) Raise your right hand so it is above and to the right of your head. Your palm should be facing the dog and your fingers should be pointing up. The dog should go down as soon as he sees this signal and should stay down until you begin step (5).

(5) Instruct your dog to sit by rapidly moving your right hand from its customary position to eye level. When you do this, cup your hand as if you were holding a softball; and swing your hand upward as if you were throwing the ball in the air.

(6) Give your dog the command signal for "come." To do this, hold your right hand at shoulder level with your fingers pointing away from your body and the heel of your hand turned down. Your right arm should be straight. Motion your dog to approach you by sweeping your right hand toward your left shoulder.

This is a beckoning gesture that should cause your dog to arise from his sitting position and to move briskly in your direction. When he is in front of your feet, he will stop and assume a straight sit.

(7) Instead of giving the command "heel" to finish the exercise, move your left hand in a semicircular arc from front to rear. While you are doing this, you can pretend that you are holding the lead and

that you are guiding your dog from in front of your feet to the heel position. Your fingers should be pointing at the ground and your hand should remain at the same level—it should not move up or down. At the widest part of the arc, your hand should be about twelve inches to the left of your body.

After this final cue, your dog will remain at your side until the person in charge indicates that the exercise is over.

In a class or competition, the leader will tell you when to give each signal. You will be instructed to "stand your dog," "leave your dog," "down your dog," and "finish the exercise." Each of these instructions must be relayed to your pet by means of a hand signal. If any signal is accompanied by a verbal command, the result will be disqualification. If a signal is not followed by a response in a specified amount of time, the penalty will be a substantial loss of points.

To teach your dog this exercise, all that is required is to make him familiar with the various hand signals. The actions that he will perform have all been included in the previous courses. Even some of the signals are not new. For example, in your previous work the gesture for "stay" has always accompanied the verbal command. You may remember that in the Novice Class it was suggested that you incorporate the hand signal in the training for the Long Down. This was recommended so that your dog would see this signal on several occasions before he was ready for Utility Work.

The Signal Exercise is not learned all at once; each signal is treated as a separate entity. To begin training, you should put your dog on leash. Do not hesitate to use the leash even though your dog is used to performing without it. When there is new material to be learned, the leash is still a valuable means of control.

The first of the five hand signals—the gesture for "stay"—will require the least explanation. In the past, you have given this signal at the same time as the verbal command. Your dog already knows what you want when he sees your left palm in front of his face with your fingers pointing down.

What you have to accomplish for this exercise is to eliminate the verbal command. This can be done by telling your dog to stay, showing him the hand signal, and circling around him as you did in the Beginner's Class. Repeat this procedure a few times and then try it with just the hand signal. If you are successful, do not eliminate the word "stay" all at once. Repeat this word every second or third time until you are sure that it is no longer necessary.

Corrective action will be needed if your dog carelessley disobeys the signal command or if he sits when he should remain standing. In the first instance, chastise your dog by tapping him lightly on the nose and by uttering the command "stay" in a firm voice. In the second instance, physically lift your dog onto his feet and scold him by saying "no" and "shame."

The hand signal for "down" was introduced in the Novice chapter although its use was not required at that time. The following procedure was suggested for teaching your dog to obey this signal:

(1) Start with the dog on lead and in the heel position.

(2) In one movement, step out in front of your dog and turn so that you are facing him.

(3) Raise your right hand above the right side of your head and simultaneously give the verbal command "down." If your dog does not respond, jerk the lead vigorously with your left hand.

(4) Repeat steps (1) through (3) and gradually eliminate the jerk on the lead and then the verbal command. In removing these cues follow the same procedure that you used to eliminate the word "stay." For example, jerk the lead one time and not the next. Continue to alternate until the use of the lead is unnecessary.

(5) When you have successfully completed step (4), remove the lead and train your dog to obey the hand signal when the two of you are further apart. To do this, give the command "stay" and leave your dog. Instead of taking one step and turning (as you did in step 2), take a few paces before you pivot. Then raise your right hand above your head and keep it aloft until your dog goes down. Once your dog is prone, praise him, return to his side, and remain there for at least a few seconds.

Each time you repeat this procedure, take a few extra steps. Continue to increase the distance between you and your dog until the two of you are separated by thirty feet. If at any time your dog does not respond to the hand signal, give him the verbal command "down" in a firm tone of voice.

The third signal that your dog should recognize is the one that motions him from the down position to a straight sit. This signal is introduced in much the same way as the signal for "down." Once again you will start with the dog on leash and in the heel position. As you did before, you will take a step forward and turn and face your dog. Your next action is to give three cues at once. Utter the command "sit," pull up on the lead with your left hand, and with your right hand make the sweeping motion that was described in the outline of the exercise.

To convert this triple command to a single command, first eliminate the spoken instruction and then do without the tug on the leash. If you are successful, have your dog respond to the hand motion several times until you are sure that he associates this signal with the act of sitting. If you are not successful, the remedy is to backtrack. Return to the use of the leash and the spoken command and keep these in your routine until you are sure that they are no longer necessary.

The fourth and fifth signals—to come and to heel—are also taught with the help of the leash and the spoken command. As your dog becomes familiar with these signals (which were described in the outline of the exercise), the actions that are not part of the exercise should be dropped. First, the spoken command should be eliminated and then the use of the leash should be discontinued.

When your dog has learned all five signals, test him by having him perform the entire exercise. Leave a gap of about ten to fifteen seconds between commands. When you are satisfied with your dog's performance, vary the sequence of commands so you are sure that he is responding to signals and not just memorizing a routine.

Signal Exercise

Stay. Place your left hand in front of the dog's face. Your palm should be turned to the dog and your fingers should be pointing down.

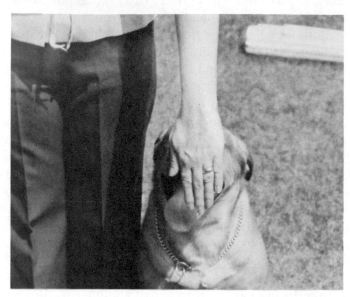

Down. Raise your right hand so it is above and to the right of your head. Your palm should be facing the dog and your fingers should be pointing up.

Sit. To raise your dog from the down position, start by cupping your right hand.

Move this hand swiftly upward to show that you want the dog to rise.

Come. Hold your right arm at shoulder level with your fingers pointing away from your body and the heel of your hand turned down.

Motion your dog to approach you by sweeping your right hand toward your left shoulder.

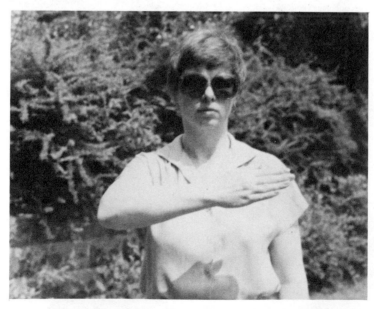

Heel. Start this command with your left hand in its customary position.

To get your dog to heel, move your hand in a semicircular arc from front to rear. At the widest part of the arc, your hand should be twelve inches to the left of your body.

DIRECTED RETRIEVE

This exercise requires two skills—selection and retrieval. The latter skill was taught in the Open Class. Selection was the important part of the Scent Discrimination exercise, where your dog learned to use his sense of smell to select the proper object out of a group of nine. The group was very compact, with approximately six inches space between adjacent objects.

In the Directed Retrieve, a selection will also be required, but this time it will be based on location rather than scent. Three objects will be used instead of nine, and the distance between the objects will be almost half the width of the ring.

The Directed Retrieve is not a difficult exercise to learn; it can be performed as follows:

(1) The handler will provide three identical work gloves that are predominantly white and are open at one end. The gloves must be made of cotton and must be shown to the person in charge before the exercise begins.

(2) At the start of the exercise, the dog will be standing next to the handler in the heel position and both will be facing a table and chair that is at one end of the ring. At the other end, the judge or steward will position the three gloves. One will be placed about three feet from the left side of the ring; one will be three feet from the right side of the ring; and the other glove will be half way between them. The middle glove will be about three feet from the far end of the ring.

(3) The handler and dog will be facing away from the area that will contain the gloves. Once the gloves are positioned, the instruction will be either "one," "two," or "three." The number that is announced indicates the location of the glove to be retrieved. "One" refers to the glove in the left corner, "two" to the center glove, and "three" to the glove at the right. When this instruction is given, the handler will tell the dog to heel and the handler and dog will turn so that they are facing the proper glove. The dog will sit in the heel position and will wait for the next command. The handler must not touch the dog or do anything to alter the dog's position.

(4) The next instruction will be "take it" or "fetch it." The handler will respond by moving his or her left hand along the right side of the dog in the direction of the glove. This gesture will either accompany or immediately precede the command to retrieve.

(5) The dog will respond to the command and signal by moving briskly to the proper glove. The glove should be picked up without any unnecessary mouthing or playing. If the wrong glove is retrieved, the dog will be automatically disqualified.

(6) As in the Retrieve on Flat, the dog will keep the object in his mouth, will return to the handler, and will stand in front of the handler's feet. The dog will not release the object until the handler gives the command "out."

After the handler has taken the glove, the person in charge will say "finish the exercise." The handler will give the command "heel" and the dog will move from in front of the handler's feet to the handler's left side.

The dog is only required to make one retrieval. The person in charge should be careful, however, to designate different glove numbers for successive dogs. Otherwise, if two dogs in a row make a retrieval in the same area, the dog who goes second will have an unfair advantage.

As you review the outline, you will note that steps (1) through (3) are merely a preparation for the performance of the exercise and step (6) is a description of a routine that your dog has already learned. Therefore, in your training sessions, you should concentrate on the actions described in steps (4) and (5).

The way to begin is to put the dog on leash and to work with only one glove. This should be placed directly in front of you and about fifteen to twenty feet from where you will start the exercise. When you are ready, walk your dog to the glove and command him to pick it up. You may have to be persistent because your dog is not accustomed to working with this type of material. If he balks at retrieving the glove, it may be necessary to look back to the section on the Retrieve on Flat—particularly at the techniques that were used to teach the dog to pick up the dumbbell.

Once the glove is in the dog's mouth, he should be guided back to the starting point and should be commanded to complete the exercise as he would in a class or competition. In other words, he should duplicate the routine that is described in step (6) of the outline. Repeat this entire procedure a few times and then see how your dog will perform without the leash.

To do this, have your dog sit next to you and have someone else position the glove. It should still be about fifteen to twenty feet directly in front of the starting point. Wait a few seconds and then give the command "fetch it" and the hand signal that was described in step (4). If your training has been successful, your dog will run directly to the object, pick it up, and retrieve it.

Do not stop training as soon as your dog has returned. Make him wait for the commands "out" and "heel," so he gains experience in performing the entire exercise. Continue to work with only one glove until your dog consistently picks it up without hesitation and releases it without resistance. When this is accomplished, your dog will have mastered the retrieval portion of the exercise. The next phase of his training should teach him how to make a selection.

As the word "selection" implies, a second object will have to be used. Another glove should be placed in the retrieval area a fair distance from the first glove and directly to its right. In other words, if you walked in a straight line from the staring point to the first glove, you would have to make a 90° right turn and walk a few steps until you reached the second glove.

Once the gloves are positioned, practice should resume and your dog should be told to fetch. The only clue he will have as to which glove to retrieve will be the direction in which he is facing when he receives the command and signal. If he starts toward the wrong glove, scold him immediately. Do not overlook any mistakes or your dog may stop paying attention and may fail to understand what is required in the exercise.

Another pitfall to avoid is forming a pattern where you consistently alternate from one glove to the other. The problem with this is that your dog may recognize what you are doing. If he does, he will base his selection on which glove he picked up last and not on the direction in which he was facing.

Success with two gloves should encourage you to add another glove to the retrieval area. This glove should be positioned to the left of the other two, so that the three objects are in a line and so the left- and right-hand gloves are both the same distance from the center glove.

The addition of a third object is the final step in training your dog to do this exercise. If your dog has been attentive, the transition from two objects to three will not be difficult.

CORRECTIVE ACTION: If your dog has trouble with this exercise, there are two things you can do to improve his performance.

(1) You can increase the angle between objects and then gradually return the objects to their original position.

(2) You can put your dog on leash and walk him to the glove he is supposed to retrieve. Do this a few times and then remove the lead, so that your dog gets the idea that you want him to retrieve the glove on his own. You can continue to alternate between the leash being on and off until your dog can perform the exercise without any assistance.

Watch your dog carefully so you can correct him if he makes a mistake. To acquaint yourself with the types of errors that judges look for, you can refer to the judge's worksheet at the end of this chapter. You can also contact the American Kennel Club and request a copy of the *A.K.C. Obedience Rules and Regulations Book.*

Directed Retrieve

To perform this exercise in competition, you will have to provide three identical white, cotton work gloves that are open at one end.

When the person in charge says "take it" or "fetch it," you should respond by moving your left hand along the right side of the dog in the direction of the glove to be retrieved.

DIRECTED JUMPING

In the High Jump in the Open Class, the dog started at the handler's side, went over a jump to retrieve a dumbbell, and with the dumbbell in his mouth he cleared the same jump to return to the handler.

This procedure is greatly modified in Directed Jumping. The most obvious difference is the presence of two jumps instead of one. The routine is also different—when the dog leaves the heel position, he must run in between the jumps, stop at a point that is twenty feet beyond them, and then turn and face the handler. The dog must sit until the handler indicates which jump he should go over. The dog will then clear the jump and return to the handler as in the retrieval exercises.

In Directed Jumping the dog is given more responsibility and there is a greater chance of error. A dog can be disqualified for any one of the following infractions: (1) anticipating *or* not obeying the command to go out; (2) not going out between the jumps or not going at least ten feet beyond them; (3) not coming to a stop and sitting when the handler gives the command "sit"; (4) anticipating or disobeying the command or signal to jump; (5) not jumping as directed; (6) knocking the bar off the uprights or using the top of the high jump as an aid to get over.

To avoid these errors may require a considerable amount of work. Before you begin training, you should review the detailed outline of the exercise that follows:

(1) The handler and dog begin the exercise in the heel position facing a high jump and bar jump that are in the center of the ring (lengthwise) and are from eighteen to twenty feet apart. The handler and dog are midway between the two jumps (from left to right) and are twenty feet away from them.

(2) Following the instruction from the judge, the handler will tell the dog to go out, and the dog will move quickly between the jumps and will continue for about twenty feet.

(3) At this point the handler will give the command "sit." The dog will stop, turn around, and will sit facing the handler. There is no penalty if the dog's sit is not exactly straight.

(4) The judge will indicate which jump is to be taken first. The handler will communicate this to the dog by giving the command "over" and by pointing to the proper jump.

(5) When the dog receives the command and signal, he will leave his sitting position and proceed to the proper jump. As the dog is clearing the jump, the handler will turn so that he or she is facing the dog. Once the dog has landed, he will run directly to the handler and come to a straight sit in front of the handler's feet.

(6) The dog will retain this position until the judge says "finish the exercise" and the handler gives the command "heel." Following this command, the dog will move to his handler's left side and will wait for the next instruction.

(7) The Directed Jumping is not completed at the end of step (6). Instead, the judge will ask "are you ready?" and if the handler's reply is "yes," the judge will instruct the handler to begin the second part of the exercise. This is a duplication of steps (2) through (6), with the only exception being that a different jump is used.

The system for determining the height of the jumps is the same as was used in the Open Class. That is, the height of each jump should be 1½ times the distance from the ground to the dog's withers, with no jump being less than eight or more than thirty six inches. The judge may select either jump to be first, but the same jump may not be taken twice. A dog must go over both obstacles to successfully complete the exercise.

The bar jump was not used in any of the previous exercises. It consists of two uprights that are about five feet apart and are linked by a single horizontal. This connecting bar is between 2 and 2½ inches from bottom to top and from front to back. The bar is painted with alternating bands of black and white, with each band approximately three inches thick. The edges of the bar are rounded to avoid sharpness. The height of the bar can be adjusted to suit the dog who is jumping.

The training for this exercise is focused on the activities that occur in steps (2) through (4)—namely, the leaving of the handler, the response to the command "sit," and the selection of the proper jump. The clearing of the jump and the return to the handler are familiar activities that do not require as much attention.

To begin practice, you will need the two jumps and a clear area that has the same dimensions as an obedience ring—roughly 35 x 50 feet. If possible, rope off this area so it resembles a ring. It is a good idea to have someone help you as you teach your dog to do this exercise.

Before your first training session, cut a square piece of white cloth and place this cloth where you will want your dog to stop when you give the command "sit." When you are ready, put your dog on leash and walk him to the starting point for the exercise—this should be approximately forty feet from the white cloth.

With your dog in the heel position and facing the cloth, give the command "go out" and point straight ahead. Then move briskly with your dog in the direction in which you pointed. You will pass in between the two jumps and will give the command "sit" as you approach the cloth. The first time you try this, help your dog into the proper position. Remember that when your dog sits he should be facing the starting point and should not be facing in the direction in which he was running.

Your dog may learn this part of the exercise faster if he is given some extra incentive for doing it right. You can encourage him by placing a small treat on the white cloth. When you do this, you may have to use the leash to keep your dog from running after the treat or from taking it before it is deserved. To earn his reward, your dog will have to perform this part of the exercise correctly. This means that he will have to respond to the command "go out," move quickly between the jumps, heed the command "sit," and turn so he is facing the starting point. When he has accomplished all this, your dog should be praised and allowed to eat.

When you are working with your dog, you should be both a trainer and an observer. As a trainer, you will have to teach your dog what needs to be done; as an observer, you will have to watch your dog carefully to make sure that he is learning. If he appears to be doing well, you should gradually remove the training aids. First, reduce the size of the cloth, then eliminate the treat, and then try the exercise without a leash. Continue to work with your dog until none of these devices are necessary.

Your dog should now be ready to start jumping. He has already learned how to jump in the Open Class, but if you want him to start slowly you can set the jumps at less than their required height.

The first time you try this part of the exercise you may want to walk your dog to his sitting place, give him the command "stay," and then return to the other side of the jumps. Your next move will be to sidestep to the left or right (depending on which jump you want your dog to clear) so you are facing the desired jump. Then point to the jump and give the command "over." Your dog should respond by clearing the barrier and by approaching you as he did in the Open Class.

When your dog is first learning this exercise, it is a good idea to have an assistant stationed on the far side of the jumps to discourage your dog from going off course. As your dog becomes familiar with Directed Jumping, some of your procedures should gradually change. (1) You will not have to accompany your dog to where he should sit. (2) You can remain in the starting place and point to the jump and not have to move close to it, as you did in the initial stages of training. (3) You can rely on your dog to go over the proper jump without using an assistant to keep him on course.

CORRECTIVE ACTION: If your dog does not obey the command "go out" or if he goes out slowly, you can attach a long leash to his choke collar and you can put this leash through a ring that is fastened to a ground stake. The loose end of the lead should be held by your assistant. When you give the command "go out," your assistant will take the lead and run away from the jumps and the sitting area instead of toward them. When you give the command "sit," your assistant will stop. After a few repetitions of this technique, your dog should be ready to perform the exercise without the use of the lead.

For other problems with this exercise, you may refer to your previous experience. Think back to the corrective measures that were suggested for the jumping and recall exercises and use these techniques as you see fit.

Directed Jumping

The bar jump. In practice, you may want to block the bottom of this jump to prevent the dog from running under.

When you tell your dog to sit, he will stop and turn so he is facing you. Each of you will be about twenty feet from the jumps.

When you give the command "over" you will have to point to the jump that the dog should take.

Once the dog clears the jump, he will run toward you and sit in front of your feet.

This exercise tests you dog's ability to retain his composure while you are away from his side and he is being examined by a judge. Your dog will perform this exercise with not less than five nor more than fourteen other dogs. The nearness of the other animals may make your dog more likely to misbehave.

From start to finish, the Group Examination is performed as follows:

(1) Contestants will position themselves side by side in catalog order so that they form a straight line that runs the length of the ring and divides the ring in half. The dogs will be sitting in the heel position. Handlers will remove their armbands and will place them (and other articles such as leashes) behind their dogs for identification.

(2) The first two instructions from the judge will be "stand your dog" and "leave your dog." Following the first instruction all handlers will stand and pose their dogs. After the second instruction handlers will give the command "stay," will walk forward to the side of the ring, and will then turn and face their dogs.

(3) The judge will proceed down the line and will examine each dog individually. This is done by approaching the dog from the front and by going over him with both hands as in a dog show—with the exception that the examination must not include the dog's mouth or testicles. While the judge is examining one dog, the stewards are observing other dogs and are making a record of any infractions.

(4) When all dogs have been examined and the handlers have been away for at least three minutes, the judge will give the order "back to your dogs." Each handler will walk back past his or her dog's left side and will circle behind the dog and come to a stop with the dog in the heel position. When this has been accomplished, the judge will indicate that the exercise is finished.

There is generally no attempt to evaluate the way in which dogs are made to stand. However, penalties will be given if the handler is rough in standing the dog or if during this period the dog is openly resistant. Outside of these exceptions, the scoring of the exercise does not begin until the judge gives the instruction "leave your dog." Dogs will be penalized if they move their feet at any time during the exercise or if

EXERCISE	NON QUALIFYING ZERO	QUALIFYING — SUBSTANTIAL	QUALIFYING — MINOR	Maximum Points	Points Lost	NET SCORE
SIGNAL EXERCISE	Handler adapting self to dog pace □; Unmanageable □; Unqualified heeling □; Any audible comm. □; Failure on first signal to: Stand □, Stay □, Drop □, Sit □, Come □; Anticipated □; Sat out of reach □	Forging □; Lagging □; No change of pace □; Heeling wide – on turns – abouts □; Extra signal to heel □; Holding signals □; Slow response to signal to Stand □ .. Down □ .. Sit □ .. Come □; No sit front-finish □; Lack of naturalness smoothness □	Crowding handler □; Sniffing □; Fast □ Slow □; Sit □; Touching handler □; Sat between feet □; Poor sits □; Poor finish □	**40**		
SCENT DISCRIMINATION	No go out 1st comm. □L □M; No retrieve □L □M; Wrong article □L □M; LEATHER: Anticipated □, Extra command □, Sat out of reach □; METAL: Anticipated □, Extra command □, Sat out of reach □	L □ M □ Handler roughness □; Sat after turn □; Doesn't work continuously □; Dropping article on return □; Mouthing □; Picks up wrong article then dropped: □; Slow response □; No sit in front □; No finish □; Handler error □	L □ M □ Touched handler □; Sat between feet □; Poor sit □; Poor finish □	LEATHER **30** / METAL **30**		
DIRECTED RETRIEVE	Does Not: Go out on command □; Go directly to glove □; Retrieve right article □; Fails to retrieve □; Anticipated □; Extra signal □; Sat out of reach □	Touching dog sending □; Excessive signals □; Slow response to command □; Mouthing □; Dropping article □; Poor delivery □; No sit in front □; No finish □; Lack of naturalness smoothness □	Playing □; Touching handler □; Sat between feet □; Poor sit □; Poor finish □	**30**		

DIRECTED JUMPING			40

HIGH JUMP
Does Not:
Leave on order...
Go substantially in right direction.
Stop on command.
Jump as directed.
Climbing jump...
Anticipated command...
Does not go at least 10' beyond jumps.

BAR JUMP
Does Not:
Leave on order...
Go substantially in right direction.
Stop on command.
Jump as directed.
Knocking bar off...
Anticipated command...
Does not go at least 10' beyond jumps.

Holding signals...
Slow response to directions...
Slightly off direction...
Not back far enough...
Anticipated □ Turn □ Stop □ Sit
Does not sit on command
No sit in front   Touched handler
No finish   Sat between feet
Lack of naturalness   Poor sits...
— smoothness   Poor finishes...

MAX. SUB-TOTAL → **170**

GROUP EXAMINATION	ZERO		30

Substantial move...
Growls or snaps...
Goes to another dog...
Sits or lies down before handler returns

Minor move away...
Shows shyness...
Resentment...
Repeated barks or whines...

Resistance to handler posing...
Moved feet slightly...
Minor whine or bark...
Sits or lies down after handler returns to heel position...

MAXIMUM POINTS → **200**

Less Penalty for Unusual Behavior ↑

□ H. Disciplining □ Shows Fear □ Fouling Ring □ Disqualified □ Expelled □ Excused

EXPLANATION OF PENALTY

TOTAL NET SCORE →

Courtesy of Ralston Purina Company.

145

they sit or lie down after the handler has returned to the heel position. Deductions will also be made if the dog exhibits any shyness or resentment while he is in the presence of the judge.

This exercise reinforces what your dog has learned in the earlier classes. In the Beginner's Course your dog first encountered the Stand for Examination. In the Novice Class the exercise was repeated without the use of the leash and the examination was conducted in greater detail. While there was no standing exercise in the Open Class, the dog had to come to a stand at the end of the Healing Off Leash. In the Utility Class standing was required as part of the Signal Exercise.

Thus, to prepare your dog for the Group Examination, you will not have to teach him anything new. All that is rcommended is that you practice standing your dog and leaving him for increasingly longer periods of time. If you have the opportunity, try to perform the exercise in the presence of other dogs and with someone acting as a judge. If you experience any difficulty, put your dog back on leash and refer to the sections on the Stand for Examination in Chapters 2 and 3.

CONCLUDING REMARKS

There is not much to add to what has already been said. A brief review of the judge's worksheet will remind you of the intricacy of these exercises and will point out the many places where a dog can make a mistake. To qualify in the Utility Course, a dog must score at least 170 points out of a possible 200.

If you have successfully completed this chapter, as far as this book is concerned, you have done it all. There are no other exercises described in this volume. However, it is still a good idea to hold an occasional practice session. This will serve as a refresher and will let your dog know that you still care.

What your dog has learned from these four courses will serve him for the rest of his life. It will make him a more obedient pet and because of this he will be a happier companion. Of course, you are aware of this or you would not have made the effort to progress so far.

Self-Evaluation

How much you have learned from this book can only be measured by the success you have with your dog. The purpose of these tests is to let you see if you remember the key information in each chapter. To test yourself, read through a quiz and either jot down or memorize your answers. Then turn to the next section where the proper responses are supplied. See how many questions you have answered correctly. If you are not satisfied with what you remember, you might want to turn back to the text and skim through a chapter again.

Another way that you can benefit from these quizzes is by simply reading the answer sections. Each one of these sections provides a brief summary of a chapter. By reading the answers, you can review what you have learned.

TEST 1: BEFORE OBEDIENCE TRAINING BEGINS

1. When you purchase a dog, what documents should you receive in addition to a bill of sale?
2. In Chapter 1, what is suggested as a minimum age for separating a puppy from its mother?
3. Why should a choke collar be three or four inches longer than a dog's neck?
4. Without using your dog, how can you practice the proper method of putting on a choke collar?
5. You should have a marrow bone on hand for your puppy's first day home. What should be done to the marrow bone before it is given to the dog?
6. Why should chicken, steak, or pork bones never be given to a dog?

7. Describe how the overnight use of a shortened leash contributes to the housebreaking of a dog.

8. When it is time for a puppy to relieve himself, why should you carry him outside instead of letting him walk?

9. While your dog is being housebroken, at what times during the day should he be kept on leash?

10. How can you tell that your puppy has been housebroken?

Answers to Test 1

(1) When you purchase a dog, try to get a written guarantee against defect or disease. Also ask for the dog's medical history report and shot records. If you are dealing with a breeder, make sure you receive pedigree papers.

(2) Puppies that are less than nine weeks old should not be separated from their mothers.

(3) The extra length makes the choke collar easy to slip on and off. It also allows room for growth.

(4) Before putting the choker on the dog, you should practice by putting it on your left wrist. If the choker is on correctly, the ring will fall when you release the lead with your right hand.

(5) The marrow bone should be boiled until it is white and hard. It can then be given to the dog.

(6) Chicken, steak, or pork bones may possibly splinter and get stuck in a dog's throat or intestines.

(7) At night the dog is leashed to a stationary object and kept close to its bed. Since a dog will seldom soil the area in which it sleeps and eats, this technique reduces the likelihood that a dog will wet or move its bowels during the night.

(8) There are two reasons for carrying a puppy outside when you are training him to be housebroken. First, you reduce the chance of his having an accident before he gets to the door. And, second, you can carry him to the exact spot where you want him to relieve himself.

(9) In between daytime outings, the dog who is being housebroken should be kept in his area but left off the leash. The leash should only be used at night or when no one is in the house.

(10) When a puppy is almost housebroken, he will signal you when he needs to go outside. He may do this by running in circles, by scratching the door, or by pacing up and down.

TEST 2: OBEDIENCE TRAINING FOR BEGINNERS

1. Dogs can be trained successfully at home, but what are two good reasons for taking your dog to a school?

2. To be ready for obedience training, a dog must have what qualifications?

3. What equipment must the handler obtain for the Beginner's Course?

4. Describe the position of your left hand when you are holding the lead with the dog in the heel position.

5. When you are helping your dog to sit, your left hand should be placed where on his body?

6. Describe the correct sitting position for a dog. Indicate the position of the dog in relation to the handler.

7. If during a practice session your dog sits incorrectly, what immediate action can you take?

8. When you leave your dog and want him to remain in place, what command and hand signal should you give?

9. When you leave your dog, with what foot should you take your first step?

10. The first time you leave your dog it is a good idea not to walk directly away from him. What should you do instead?

11. Assume that you have left your dog and are now returning. As you start back, should the dog be on your left or right? Describe the path that you must take to return to the heel position.

12. The command "heel" should be preceded by what verbal signal?

13. When you are heeling with your dog you can get him to stop by giving the command "halt." What other action can you expect as a result of this command?

14. To reverse directions when you are heeling, should you turn to the left or the right?

15. Why is it important in heeling not to slow down when you approach a turn?

16. How can you teach your dog not to forge ahead of you?

17. What corrective measures can be taken to keep your dog from heeling wide?

18. Why is it not a good idea to use people for posts when you first learn the Figure Eight?

19. What is the position of the handler and dog at the start of the Figure Eight exercise?

149

20. In addition to its normal function, how can the leash be used to train a dog to stand for examination?

21. If your dog is fidgety when he is approached by a judge in the Stand for Examination, what corrective action can be taken?

22. In the Recall exercise what should you do with the leash while your dog is approaching you? When the dog comes to a halt what should be his position?

23. When you receive the instruction "finish your dog," what command should you give?

24. Chapter 2 suggests four methods for teaching your dog to respond to the word "down." Describe the method that suits your dog best.

25. In returning to your dog after the Long Down, why is it a good idea to stand at his side for a few seconds and then leave?

Answers to Test 2

(1) If you attend a school, your dog can be observed by a qualified instructor and can learn to obey your commands in the presence of other animals.

(2) To start obedience training, a dog must be housebroken and must have received a shot for rabies. The minimum starting age may vary from 4½ to 6 months, depending on the requirements of the school or instructor.

(3) The only equipment needed for the Beginner's Course is a six-foot leash and a choke collar. The width of the leash will depend on the size of the dog.

(4) When your dog is in the heel position, your left hand should be on the leash about eight to ten inches away from the choke collar. Your left palm should be turned to the rear.

(5) To get your dog to sit, put your left hand on the dog's back—as close to the tail as possible—and push down. This is a sensitive spot on young puppies, so you shouldn't push too hard.

(6) To be in the correct sitting position, the dog should be close to your left side, his back should be straight, and his front and hind legs should be aligned.

(7) If your dog sits incorrectly during practice, you can use your free left hand to alter his position. If necessary, you can also pull up with the leash to lift your dog's head.

(8) The word "stay" tells your dog to remain in place. At the same time that you give this command, your left hand should be moved in front of the dog's face so that your palm is directly in his line of sight. Your palm should be turned to the dog and your fingers should be pointing down.

(9) After you've told your dog to stay, start off on your right foot. If you make a mistake and start with your left, the dog may think that you want him to heel and he may walk with you.

(10) The first time you leave your dog, walk around him counterclockwise and repeat the commands "sit" and "stay." Continue to circle your dog until you are separated from him by the full length of the leash.

(11) When you walk back after the Long Sit, you will be facing your dog and he will be on your left side. To return to the heel position, you will have to walk past your dog and circle behind him.

(12) The command "heel" should be preceded by the dog's name. This will help you to attract the dog's attention.

(13) When you and your dog have come to a complete halt, your dog is expected to sit.

(14) To reverse directions, always turn to the right and take two steps before completing your turn. By taking these extra steps, you will be turning in an arc instead of doing an abrupt about face.

(15) If you slow down when you are approaching a turn, your dog may think that he is supposed to stop and may sit instead of turning.

(16) Forging can usually be corrected by the persistent use of the leash. If this is not sufficient, pull back on the leash with your left hand and turn into the dog's path. As you do this, use your right knee to bump the dog in the face or nose.

(17) The corrective action for heeling wide is to wrap the lead around your left leg in the vicinity of your knee. With the dog on the shortened lead, take a series of fast steps and then a series of short steps.

(18) When you first try the Figure Eight it is not a good idea to use people for posts because your dog is likely to be distracted.

(19) The Figure Eight exercise begins with the handler and dog in the heel position, halfway between the two posts, which are eight feet apart. The handler and dog are facing ahead so that one post is at their left and the other is at their right.

(20) When you are training your dog to stand for examination, you can loop the end of the leash around the dog's stomach. The balance of the leash will form a straight line from the loop to the choke collar. You can lift up on this line to raise the dog into a standing position. Another alternative is to knot the loop so that the dog thinks that he is tied in place. This will generally keep the dog from moving.

(21) If your dog is fidgety during a judge's examination, you can correct him by making his training more rigorous. When you practice at home arrange to have two or three people approach your dog, touch him, and circle around him. Once your dog becomes accustomed to these people, it is unlikely that he will feel ill at ease in the presence of a single examiner.

(22) As your dog approaches you in the Recall exercise, roll or fold the leash with both hands. By the time the dog is at your feet, the entire leash should be in your right hand and this hand should be close to the choke collar. The dog should stop directly in front of you and should assume a straight sit.

(23) The instruction "finish your dog" should be followed by the command "heel." The dog will leave his sitting position in front of your feet and will move to his customary place at your left side. This position must be held until the exercise is over.

(24) The size of your dog may determine the method that you choose to train your dog to lie down. If you don't recall the methods presented in Chapter 2, please refer to pages 48-50.

(25) The purpose of returning to your dog twice is to prevent him from breaking early. After you have done this a few times, when you return to him he will not be able to anticipate if you are going to stay or leave. Because of this, he will not change his position until he receives your command. This technique is only used in practice.

TEST 3:   THE NOVICE CLASS
IN DOG OBEDIENCE

1. A tight lead is a danger sign when you perform the Figure Eight. What does the tight lead usually indicate?
2. During the Stand for Examination some dogs will lick the examiner's hand. What is a good way to discourage this?
3. Chapter 3 suggests three interim steps between heeling on lead and heeling free. Can you describe the procedures that should be followed before you are ready to work without the leash?
4. When your dog is learning to heel free in what type of places should you hold your practice sessions?
5. Name one of the three things to remember about your left hand when you are practicing heeling without the leash.
6. How should you respond if your dog runs away from you during practice?
7. What techniques can be used to discourage your dog from running away?
8. After the dog has stopped in front of the handler in the Recall exercise, the dog and handler should be how far apart?
9. During the training for the Recall exercise, the lead should be taken off the dog but should not be put away. What is the function of the leash after it has been detached?

10. In the Novice Class, the distance for the Recall exercise is increased from six to thirty feet. What steps should be taken to help the dog make this transition?

11. Describe a way that you can tempt your dog to respond to the command "come."

12. How can you teach your dog not to anticipate the command "heel" at the end of the Recall exercise?

13. In what ways is the Long Sit more difficult in the Novice Class than it was in the Beginner's Course?

14. Describe the hand signal that has the same meaning as the command "down."

15. To qualify in the Long Down in the Novice Class, the dog must hold his position for three minutes. How can this three-minute period be used productively in practice?

Answers to Test 3

(1) A tight lead usually indicates that a dog is either lagging or forging.

(2) Hand-licking in the Stand for Examination can be discouraged through the use of the following procedure: In practice have the person who examines your dog wear two white gloves. One should be moistened with water, sprinkled with pepper, and allowed to dry. The other glove should be saturated with white vinegar and should be worn on the hand that touches the dog.

(3) The first step in the transition from heeling on lead to heeling free is to stretch the lead across your chest and to place the loose end over your right shoulder. After you do this, let go with both hands and start to practice. The second step is to drop the lead on the ground so that it will trail alongside the dog. The third step is to detach the lead but to keep it in your hand where the dog can see it.

(4) To prevent your dog from running away when he is learning to heel free, hold your practice sessions indoors or in an enclosed area. Possible training sites are a garage, a basement, a courtyard, or a fenced in tennis court or baseball field.

(5) When you are practicing heeling, keep your left hand away from the dog so that you don't force him to heel wide. While you are heeling, you may want to keep cadence by tapping your left thigh. If when you come to a halt your dog sits incorrectly, you can use your left hand to modify his position.

(6) If your dog runs away from you during practice, do not chase after him. The best way to get him back is to start moving quickly in the opposite direction and to call his name and coax him to return.

(7) To discourage your dog from running away, put him on lead and let the lead trail along the ground. If your dog tries to get away, step firmly on the lead to prevent him from escaping. Another way to prevent him from wandering is to keep small pieces of meat cupped in your left hand and to keep this hand close to your dog's nose and mouth.

(8) When the dog sits in front of you in the Recall exercise, there should be no contact between the two of you. The dog should be close enough for you to reach out and touch.

(9) After you remove the lead, stretch it out on the ground so that it forms a straight line from your dog's feet to the place where he will finish the exercise.

(10) To train your dog to come to you from a distance of thirty feet, replace the six-foot lead with a lead that is thirty feet long. This new piece of equipment should be placed on the ground and should be parallel to the path that your dog will take when you give the command "come." The first time that you work with the new lead, you should only unroll the first ten feet. This will be the distance between you and your dog when you call him. If your dog responds correctly, you can repeat the exercise and increase the length of the lead.

(11) To get your dog to respond to the command "come," you may have to give him some extra encouragement. Sometimes a few words of praise are sufficient. Other times you may have to tempt your dog with a freshly cooked piece of meat.

(12) You can prevent your dog from anticipating the command "heel" at the end of the Recall exercise. To do this, put your dog on leash and stand in front of him. Walk backwards for a few paces and then come to an abrupt stop. On one occasion you should follow this stop with the command "heel." On the next few occasions you should wait for your dog to sit and you should then continue to walk backwards. By varying the routine, you will prevent your dog from forming a pattern. He will have to wait for your command to know what he is supposed to do.

(13) The Novice version of the Long Sit is more difficult than the Beginner's version in that the exercise is performed without a leash and the separation between the handler and the dog is increased from six to thirty feet. These conditions are made even more difficult by the fact that on some occasions as many as fifteen dogs will perform this exercise at the same time.

(14) The hand signal for "down" is the raising of the right hand above the right side of the head. When this signal is given the right palm should be turned to the dog and the fingers should be pointing up. The hand should be lifted straight up and should not be in front of the body.

(15) In practice you can use the three-minute down period to see how your dog reacts to praise. While he is lying down, you can shower him with continuous encouragement and note his response. Some dogs require a steady stream of compliments. Other dogs will misbehave if they are over-praised.

TEST 4: *THE OPEN COURSE*

1. In the Drop on Recall some dogs will creep forward after they receive the command "down." What corrective action can be taken to eliminate this habit?
2. How can you prevent your dog from anticipating the command "down" in the Drop on Recall?
3. What are the considerations in selecting a dumbbell for the retrieval exercises?
4. When you are teaching your dog to retrieve why should you avoid using household items such as socks, slippers, or clothes?
5. What should you do if your dog fails to respond to the command "fetch"?
6. Suppose that you are walking your dog through the Retrieve on Flat and he makes no effort to pick up the dumbbell. Describe the procedure that you should use for inserting the dumbbell in his mouth.
7. After taking the corrective action that is referred to in question 6, how can you teach your dog to hold onto the dumbbell?
8. How can you train your dog to bring back the dumbbell after he has learned to fetch it?
9. What command prompts the dog to release the dumbbell? What action follows this command?
10. In the Retrieve Over High Jump what is the ideal landing place for the dumbbell? How is the height of the jump determined?
11. What should you do to help your dog when he first goes over the high jump?
12. How can you correct your dog if he runs around the high jump instead of going over it?
13. In the Broad Jump the first instruction is "leave your dog." The handler will respond to this by giving the command "stay" and by moving to what new position?
14. How does the position of the handler change after the dog has cleared the broad jump?

15. Explain how to determine the distance of the broad jump and the number of hurdles used to create the jump.

16. What preliminary training should take place before your dog tries to jump the distance that is required in competition?

17. Describe the corrective action that will help the dog who remains in place when he hears the command "over."

18. What can the handler do to correct a dog who is scraping or grazing hurdles? How can the handler prevent the dog from jumping hurdles at an angle?

19. What is a possible reason for a dog failing to heel at the end of the Broad Jump exercise?

20. Why is the Long Sit more difficult in the Open Class than it was in the previous courses?

21. When the Long Sit is performed in a competition what position do the handlers take when they *return* to the ring?

22. How can you train your dog to remain seated when you are not in his presence?

23. What type of error should you anticipate when you are practicing with your dog and you try to leave the room?

24. What faults in the Retrieve Over High Jump would cause a dog to be disqualified?

25. If a dog scores less than half the points that are available in an exercise, can he still accumulate enough points in the other exercises to gain his title?

Answers to Test 4

(1) If your dog creeps forward when he is supposed to be lying down, walk quietly toward him and tap him on the nose with the back of your hand. As you do this, give him the command "down" in a firm tone of voice.

(2) You can prevent your dog from anticipating the command "down" by varying your routine in practice. When your dog approaches you, sometimes motion him to lie down and other times let him come to your feet without interruption. By being inconsistent, you will prevent your dog from forming a pattern. Instead of making a habit of lying down in the middle of his approach, he will keep walking until he receives your command.

(3) The dumbbell you select for your dog should be made of light wood and should be wide enough so that it doesn't interfere with the dog's vision. The rod that joins the two bells should be high enough so that the dog can pick up the dumbbell without putting his nose on the ground.

(4) If you have your dog retrieve household items, he will get used to holding these items in his mouth and he may revert to chewing.

(5) To correct a dog who doesn't respond to the command "fetch," put the dog on leash and walk him to the dumbbell. As you are walking, repeat the command.

(6) If when you are walking through the Retrieve on Flat your dog makes no effort to retrieve the dumbbell, you will have to place the dumbbell in his mouth. To do this, pick up the dumbbell in your left hand without letting go of the leash. Move this hand closer to the choke collar so that the dog is near your side. Put the thumb and forefinger of your right hand on the dog's lower lip behind the incisor teeth. Push down gently, to open the dog's mouth, and insert the dumbbell.

(7) To teach your dog to hold the dumbbell, keep your right hand under the dog's mouth to prevent him from dropping the dumbbell or spitting it out. Repeat the words "hold it" or "keep it" and heel around the area. Stop every twenty feet and insist that the dog continue to hold the dumbbell; then continue heeling.

(8) You can use the following technique to train your dog to bring back the dumbbell. When the dog picks up the dumbbell, step out in front of him and start to walk backwards. After a few steps, stop and help the dog into a straight sit. Do this a few times until you reach the place where the exercise started. At this spot, pause for fifteen seconds, give the command "out," and reach for the dumbbell.

(9) The command "out" will prompt the dog to release the dumbbell. After the dumbbell is with the handler, the dog should retain his sitting position until he receives the command "heel."

(10) In the Retrieve Over High Jump, the ideal landing spot for the dumbbell is twelve to fifteen feet beyond the high jump and in line with the center of the jump. The height of the jump is determined by measuring the distance from the ground to the dog's withers and multiplying this distance by $1\frac{1}{2}$. No jump may be less than eight inches or more than thirty six inches.

(11) To teach your dog to go over the barrier, put him on lead and walk quickly to the jump. Hesitate as you approach the jump and give the command "hup" or "over." To let your dog know what he is supposed to do, step over the jump with him.

(12) If your dog runs around the jump, get people to stand at either end of it. These people will scold your dog if he starts to run off course. Another alternative is to set up the jump in a narrow area where there is no extra space to the left or right.

(13) In the Broad Jump, after you give the command "stay," walk to the right side of the jump and turn so you are facing it. You should be two feet from the jump and should be anywhere between the first and last hurdles.

(14) After the dog goes over the jump, you should turn 90° to the right so you are facing in the direction in which the dog just jumped. The dog will do an about turn and come toward you.

(15) The distance that the dog must jump is equal to twice the height that is expected of him in the high jump. The number of hurdles to be used is dependent on the length of the jump.

(16) Before your dog attempts the Broad Jump, put one hurdle on top of another to create an obstacle. Directly behind the obstacle you can place the remaining hurdles. Once this is done, put your dog on leash and walk him to the jump. As you approach the jump, give the command "hup," jerk the lead slightly, and go over the obstacle with your dog.

(17) If your dog does not respond to the command "over," put him on leash, rebuild the obstacle, and go over it with him again. Then return to the starting point, give the command "stay," and move to the far side of the obstacle. Call your dog and coax him to jump over the obstacle and come to you. If he balks at doing this, tug the leash gently.

(18) If your dog is scraping or grazing a hurdle, insert the obstacle between the first and second hurdles. Put the dog back on leash and help him over the jump. The presence of the obstacle will cause the dog to change his trajectory and get extra height and distance. You can use this technique to prevent the dog from jumping at an angle. To correct this problem, you should also place your right foot in front of the last hurdle.

(19) Failing to heel after the Broad Jump is sometimes the result of the handler being too close to the jump.

(20) The Long Sit becomes more difficult in the Open Class, because the length of the sit is increased to three minutes and during this period the handler is completely out of sight.

(21) In a competition all the handlers will return to the ring at the same time and will form a straight line facing the dogs. The handlers and dogs will be separated by the full width of the ring.

(22) To teach your dog to remain seated while you are out of sight, give your dog the command "stay" and move to a place where he can't see you. Return shortly and see if your dog has moved. The next step is to leave your dog and to move to a spot where you can observe his behavior without being detected. If you see your dog move, you should scold him immediately.

(23) Many dogs will follow their handlers when their handlers try to leave the room. Another common—but undesirable—response is for the dog to bark as soon as the handler has exited.

(24) A dog will be disqualified in the Retrieval Over High Jump if he refuses to respond to the command "fetch it," if he fails to clear the jump in either direction, if he leaves the handler before the command, or if he sits too far from the handler after he has retrieved the dumbbell.

(25) Gaining less than half the points in an exercise automatically disqualifies a dog for an entire competition.

TEST 5: THE UTILITY CLASS

1. Describe the articles that are used in the Scent Discrimination exercise.
2. After your scent is on the article to be retrieved by the dog, how should you hand this article to the judge?
3. Following the instruction "send your dog," what three things should you do?
4. When you train your dog for the Scent Discrimination exercise, why is it a good idea to use three types of objects instead of two?
5. The first time you practice Scent Discrimination with your dog how should the scented article be positioned in relation to the other articles?
6. How can you remove your scent from the articles that you use to practice Scent Discrimination?
7. Describe the hand signal that you should use to raise your dog from a lying to a sitting position.
8. What hand signal should you use when you want your dog to come?
9. In the Signal Exercise what hand signal should be given after the judge says "finish the exercise"?
10. What should you do if your dog sits when you give him the command or signal for "stay"?
11. Describe the articles that are used in the Directed Retrieve. Where are these articles positioned?
12. What do the numbers "one," "two," and "three" refer to in the Directed Retrieve?
13. If in practice your dog has trouble with the Directed Retrieve, what two things can you do to improve his performance?
14. Describe the position of the jumps in Directed Jumping.
15. In Directed Jumping how should the dog respond to the command "go out"?
16. What should the handler do when the dog clears either the high jump or the bar jump?
17. How can a piece of white cloth help you prepare your dog for Directed Jumping?
18. What corrective measure should be used if your dog does not respond to the command "go out"?
19. Under ordinary circumstances when does the scoring of the Group Examination begin?

20. In the Group Examination when will the judge send the handlers back to their dogs? How should the handlers respond to the judge's instruction?

Answers to Test 5

(1) For the Scent Discrimination exercise you will need two sets of articles. Each set must contain five identical objects that are clearly numbered and that are not more than six inches long. One set must be made of rigid metal; the other must be made of leather and should have nothing but leather visible with the exception of a few strands of metal or material that are needed to keep the article intact.

(2) When you give the scented article to a judge, you should place the article on the judge's clipboard or worksheet. It is important that you are the only one to touch this article or other people's scents will be mixed with your own.

(3) When you are told to send your dog in the Scent Discrimination exercise, cup your left hand over the dog's nose so he becomes familiar with your scent. Make an about turn so that you and your dog are facing the retrieval area and give your dog the command "find it."

(4) It is a good idea to use an extra set of objects when you train your dog for Scent Discrimination. This is because the use of extra items will increase your dog's discriminatory power and will prepare your dog to accept items that are not made of metal or leather.

(5) When you first train your dog to select a scented article out of a group of articles, you should place the scented article on the outside of the group rather than in the center. The distance between the group and the article to be retrieved should be reduced each time you practice.

(6) To remove your scent from the articles that you use to practice Scent Discrimination, wash these articles frequently with soap and water. After each washing, articles should be allowed to dry in the sun for eight to ten hours.

(7) To raise your dog from a sitting to a lying position, cup your right hand as if you were holding a softball. Then swing this hand straight up from its customary position at your side. At the end of this motion your hand should be at eye level.

(8) To give the hand signal for "come," hold your right hand at shoulder level with your fingers pointing toward the dog and the heel of your hand turned down. Your right arm should be straight. Motion your dog to approach you by sweeping your right hand toward your left shoulder.

(9) When the judge says "finish the exercise" make a semicircular arc with your left hand. When you give this signal your fingers should be pointing down and your hand should be moving from front to back.

(10) If your dog sits when you give him the command "stay," physically lift your dog onto his feet and scold him by saying "no" and "shame."

(11) Three identical cotton work gloves are needed for the Directed Retrieve. These gloves should be predominantly white and should be open at one end. One glove should be three feet from the left side of the ring, one should be three feet from the right side of the ring, and the third glove should be midway between the other two and should be three feet from the far end of the ring.

(12) The numbers "one," "two," and "three" refer to the left, center, and right-hand gloves, respectively.

(13) If your dog has trouble when he practices the Directed Retrieve, you can increase the angle between objects or you can put your dog on leash and walk him to the object that he is supposed to pick up.

(14) For Directed Jumping a high jump and bar jump are in the center of the ring (lengthwise) and are from eighteen to twenty feet apart.

(15) After the handler says "go out," the dog will run quickly between the two jumps and will continue for about twenty feet until he receives the command "sit."

(16) As the dog clears a jump, the handler should turn so that he or she is facing the dog.

(17) In your first training session for Directed Jumping, a white piece of cloth should be placed where the dog will be expected to sit. As encouragement for your dog a small treat can be left on the cloth.

(18) If your dog does not respond to the command "go out" or if he goes out slowly, you can attach a long leash to his choke collar and you can puts this leash through a ring that is fastened to a ground stake. The loose end of the lead should be held by your assistant. When you give the command "go out," your assistant will take the lead and will run away from the jumps instead of toward them.

(19) The scoring of the Group Examination usually does not begin until the judge says "leave your dog." However, a dog may be graded on the way he is posed if the handler is rough in standing him or if the dog is openly resistant.

(20) In the Group Examination the judge will give the order "back to your dogs" after all dogs have been examined and after the handlers have been away for at least three minutes. When the handler returns to the dog, he or she will walk past the dog's left side and will circle behind the dog and come to a stop with the dog in the heel position.

Corrective Actions
for Everyday Problems

[*Publisher's note:* When Jim Bennett taught obedience training, he concluded every class with an informal session of questions and answers. While some students used this period to discuss problems they were having with the exercises, many other people raised questions concerning everyday canine behavior. To answer these questions, Jim referred to his own experience. He also kept a record of the problems that were discussed most frequently, so he could offer solutions to these problems in his book.

For the reader's convenience, he gave these problems titles and arranged them in alphabetical order. While he died before he completed this chapter, Jim Bennett left behind some valuable information for every dog owner.]

BARKING: The old adage says "A barking dog will not bite." Whether or not this is true is the subject of some controversy, but there is no question that a dog who barks too much (regardless of his biting habits) is a source of annoyance to his owner.

In dealing with this problem you must first realize that not all barking is undesirable. You *do* want your pet to be a watchdog and to alert you if something is wrong. What you are trying to eliminate is the barking that occurs for the wrong reason. For example, some dogs bark because they don't want to be left alone. If your dog has that problem, you can correct him with the same technique that was used to teach the Long Sit in the Open Class.

As you may recall from Chapter 4, a dog is introduced to this exercise by being left alone in a room. The handler waits outside the room and returns at regular intervals to make sure that the dog hasn't moved. If the handler is only interested in discouraging barking, he or she should wait until the dog starts to make noise and should then enter the room and either scold or punish the dog. This routine should be continued until the dog can be left by himself for three minutes without disturbing the peace.

Some dogs bark or whine as a means of getting what they want. If your dog behaves this way, he is acting like a spoiled child and it is necessary for you to be very firm. Don't weaken and give him what he wants just to shut him up. Keep saying "no" and when your dog finally gets the idea and stops his barking, then he can get his reward.

BATHING: Getting your dog into the tub will not be a problem if you introduce him to bathing the same way you introduced him to the obedience exercises. Gently coax him into the tub and while he is getting in give him your encouragement. Once your dog is ready to be washed either stand him or sit him, depending on which way it is easier for you to work.

It is not a good idea to bathe a dog before he is a year old, because puppies are highly susceptible to colds and respiratory illness. Rather than put a young dog in the tub, it is safer for you to clean him with a wet towel. You can dampen the towel with either witch hazel or alcohol provided that you are careful to keep either substance out of the dog's eyes.

BLADDER AND BOWEL CONTROL: As your dog becomes housebroken, he learns to relieve himself at the proper time and in the proper place. However, if he is going to be away from home for an extended period of time, he may require your assistance. Make sure he has a chance to eliminate wastes before you go. Refrain from giving him food or water for at least two hours before you leave the house. These procedures should be followed when you are going to the vet, an obedience class, or the home of a friend.

CARS, BEHAVIOR IN: For humans a car is a second home, but for dogs a ride in an automobile means sitting still for a long time in a confined space—and that isn't easy. While a dog's misbehavior in a car is understandable, it is also dangerous and must be corrected. The commands "down" and "sit" will be helpful if your dog starts to annoy you while you're driving. To make sure these commands are heeded, you should carry a paper lunch bag with you and blow this up before you leave home. If your dog starts to get frisky and does not obey your command, either tap him or threaten him with the paper bag. Getting hit with the bag is not painful, but it startles the dog and makes him behave. Sometimes just waving the bag in the dog's direction will do the job.

After a few excursions with your dog and the paper bag, you will find that you need the bag less and less. However, it is still a good idea to keep it with you as a precaution. You may find it particularly helpful when you stop to pay a toll—especially if your dog considers toll takers to be intruders and snaps or barks at them when they take your change.

When you are driving, always keep a window partially open—even if your car is air conditioned. Just a slight stream of fresh air coming into the car may keep your dog from feeling ill at ease.

CARS, SICKNESS IN: Car sickness can sometimes be alleviated by getting your dog accustomed to the car before he takes his first trip. To do this, first let him sit in the car for a few minutes while the motor is off. If he seems relaxed and comfortable, wait for the next day and then test him in a parked car with the motor running. If there are still no ill effects, he should be ready for a ride around the block. If, however, your dog still gets car sick, it is best that you consult your veterinarian.

CHASING: Almost all dogs have a tendency to pursue moving objects. This instinct was important long ago when dogs had to hunt to obtain their foot. But today, when dogs are domestic pets, chasing is a pastime that should be discouraged—there is too much chance of the dog being injured or injuring or annoying someone else.

To control chasing, you should work hard with your dog on the commands "stay" and "come," which were discussed in Chapter 2. You should also refer to page 169 and train your dog to stay within your property lines.

While these are good general precautions, there may be a few objects that have so strong an attraction for your dog that he will disobey your commands or forget his training to remain on your property. If this is your experience, some special conditioning may be required. The following paragraphs will show you how to discourage your pet from chasing animals, bicycles, and cars.

Animals. A dog may pursue another animal to play, to have sex, or to show his superiority by intimidating the other creature. The first motive is usually not strong enough to be a problem with a well-trained dog. If your dog leaves your side due to the second or third motive, your best reaction is to join the pursuit. Since your dog will be concentrating on the other animal, he will not be aware of your proximity and he will not try to elude you. Once the other animal is captured, cornered, treed, or frightened into a place of refuge, your dog will be still. This is your opportunity to grab your dog and give him a sharp slap—underneath the side of the chin is a good place for this blow since it will startle the dog and not do any damage. The surprise of this reprimand—more than its severity—will make a lasting impression on your dog. Remember, it is important to catch him in the act. If you wait for him to return, the effect of this punishment will not be the same.

Bicycles. Cyclists are frequently chased by dogs—just ask the person who delivers your newspapers. If your dog is a bicycle chaser, make arrangements in advance for someone to come near you on a bicycle. Prepare for this person's arrival by purchasing a water gun and filling it with a solution of vinegar and water. If your dog starts to chase the bicycle, squirt him in the mouth with a few drops of the solution and scold him by saying "no" and "shame."

Cars. Dogs who chase automobiles sometimes believe that they are scaring them away. If your dog develops this habit, you can correct him in a few ways—you can use the water pistol as it was used to discourage bicycle chasing. You can have someone drive slowly by and toss tin cans at the dog if he starts to pursue the car. (The cans should not hit the dog, but the clatter of metal striking the pavement should startle the dog and cause him to change directions.) You can also arrange to be a passenger in a car that cruises by your home. (Of course, this cannot be the family car or the dog may recognize it.) When the dog starts to pursue the vehicle, instruct the driver to hit the brakes. Get out of the car and give the dog a severe tongue lashing. As a result of this method, your dog may think twice about chasing cars in the future. When he wants to run after a passing vehicle, he will hesitate for fear that you may be in it.

CHEWING: The surest way for your pet to become an unwelcome visitor is to have him damage your furniture and personal property by chewing. While this is a distressing problem, it is something that you can avoid if you plan for it ahead of your dog's arrival. What I recommend is that you get a marrow bone from your butcher and that you boil this until it is very hard. Then give the bone to the dog so he can bite on it whenever he feels the urge to chew.

If this is not the entire solution to your problem, you can also discourage chewing by coating the legs of your furniture with a mixture of vinegar and water. Any time your dog is caught chewing an object, he should be scolded and put on the short leash, as described in Chapter 1.

FEEDING YOUR DOG AT THE TABLE: If you look forward to relaxation at mealtime, this is one habit that you shouldn't encourage. That doesn't mean that you can't occasionally share your food with the family pet, but when you treat your dog to table food he should receive his portion in his own dish. If this pattern is followed conscientiously, it will keep your dog from nudging you under the table and begging for extra handouts.

If your dog is already accustomed to joining you at mealtime, you can gain a few minutes peace by giving the command "down." Your dog should lie down and remain still as soon as he hears this command. Any problems in gaining this response should prompt you to return to Chapter 2 and review the Long Down.

FIGHTING: While some dogs look for fights with other dogs, most battles between canines are caused by the anxiety of an owner. For example, a few weeks ago I watched two dogs playing in a back yard— one was the family pet and the other was a wanderer from somewhere else in the neighborhood. The two got along fine until the lady of the house looked out and yelled to the stranger to get away. The threatening tone of her voice had an immediate effect on the behavior of her dog. While before he had been playful, he now became angry, snapped at the visitor, and chased him off the lawn.

The point is that your attitude toward other dogs can be transmitted to your own pet. He will become aggressive if he is aware of the fact that you consider other dogs to be possible sources of trouble. Therefore, to control fighting you may have to control your own reactions.

If your behavior is not responsible for your dog's tendency to fight, you will have to correct him vigorously at an early age. Otherwise, the alternative is to keep him isolated and to put a "beware of dog" sign in front of your house.

FOOD, TAKEN FROM DOG WHILE EATING: Without intending to be mean, children will sometimes remove food from a dog who is eating. If this happens to your dog, you want to be confident that he will not become vicious. The only way to be sure of his reaction is to practice with him before an incident occurs.

Training Equipment: Choke collar, lead, and heavy gloves.

Training Period: Practice with your dog two or three times during every meal until you are satisfied with your dog's response.

Desired Result: Your dog will permit any member of the family to take away his food.

Teacher's Tip: Start this training when your dog is less than six months old.

When you start to train your dog, his reaction may be more violent than you anticipate. For this reason there are three precautions that are worth remembering: You should keep your dog on lead; you should wear heavy gloves; and you should keep your face a safe distance from the dog.

Training should take place during the dog's mealtime. Grab food from the dog's dish as he is about to eat. As you do this, make sure that you are watching him. If he growls, snaps, or shows any indication of temper, you should scold your dog by saying "no" and "shame." If he attempts to bite you, yank the leash so that his face is pulled away from your body.

After you have held the food for about ten seconds, return it to the dish. With your other hand, pat your dog on the head and praise him by saying "good boy."

Repeat this exercise during every meal until your dog will consistently permit you to take his food. When this has been accomplished, you can let another adult in your household try the same procedure. If this person is successful, the next one to perform the exercise should be a child.

For this operation, extra precautions are needed. You should be holding the lead and you should be prepared to restrain the dog if he moves toward the child. If there are no bad incidents in three or four trials, you can assume that the dog has been successfully trained.

A dog will usually learn the proper response in just two or three days. If, however, your pet consistently growls or snaps at the person taking his food, a stronger deterrent is needed. It may be necessary to give your dog a firm slap underneath the mouth. This is important because if his behavior is not corrected, it is likely to grow worse.

GUMMING: Has your dog ever taken your arm or leg in his mouth and held it without biting? This action, which I call "gumming," is a sign of affection or playfulness. However, it must be discouraged.

If your dog tries to gum your arm, the right response is to say "no" and to wait for your dog to open his mouth. Do not try to move your arm until the dog's mouth is open; otherwise, you are likely to tear your skin on the dog's sharp teeth.

While you can learn to live with a dog who gums, it is not a good idea to tolerate this habit. A dog who gums his owner is likely to treat a visitor in the same way. If this person doesn't know the dog, he or she may panic and may react improperly. Rather than take a chance on someone getting hurt, it is better to teach your dog that gumming is wrong.

HOUSEBREAKING: The method of housebreaking that I prefer is described in detail in Chapter 1. You will probably find this method successful provided that you stick with it conscientiously.

IDENTIFICATION: While dognapping is not a widespread crime, dogs that are obviously well trained and well bred have a high market value and may be subject to theft. Because of this, some dog owners have taken the precaution of having their social security number tattooed on their dog. In cases where the tattoo is visible, it serves as a deterrent. In cases where the tattoo cannot be seen unless the dog's coat is brushed aside, the social security number serves as a means of identification in the event that a stolen dog is recovered.

LONELINESS AT NIGHT: If your dog barks or whines at night, it is probably because he is lonely. A little puppy left alone can sound just as unhappy as a small child who is lost. If you are like most people, you will be tempted to pick up your dog, cuddle him, and take him back to your room. However, while this reaction seems humane, it is not advisable. By picking up your dog, you are encouraging him to bark or whine whenever he wants your attention. By taking him to your room, you are creating a habit that you may someday want to break. Your dog will outgrow his loneliness in a few days, but he may never want to relinquish his place in your room.

While it is not a good idea to pamper your dog, there are things you can do to make him feel better. For example, the warmth of a hot water bottle at night may remind the pup of when he slept with his mother and may make him more content. Sometimes a loud ticking clock (which sounds like a heartbeat) will have the same effect.

MEDICINES, ADMINISTERING: If your dog is not cooperative, giving him medicine will be a two-person job. One person will have to open the dog's mouth, using the technique that was described in the section on Retrieve on Flat in Chapter 4. The other person will insert the medicine.

Once the pill or liquid has been inserted, the dog's mouth will have to be shut so that the medicine does not spill out. If you are giving your dog a pill, put it far back on his tongue. This way he will be forced to swallow it as soon as his mouth is closed.

Some dogs may be able to hold medicine in their mouth and spit it out after their mouth is opened. To prevent this, you should keep the dog's mouth shut for at least a minute. While you are doing this, stroke the dog's throat to encourage him to swallow.

NOISE, ADVERSE REACTIONS TO: Overreacting to loud noises is a trait that some pups acquire at birth and others develop soon afterwards. If you notice this tendency in your dog and try to shelter him from unpleasant sounds, his condition will grow worse. You will help him more if you can get him accustomed to loud noises—perhaps by associating them with events that he enjoys.

With this purpose in mind, a friend of mine would call his dog to dinner by firing a cap pistol. At first, the dog would cringe at the sound of the gun. But he soon learned to accept it because it signalled the start of his dinner. From this experience the dog learned to tolerate other loud noises, such as the backfiring of a car or the thunder of an electrical storm.

PROPERTY, STRAYING FROM: A dog who leaves his home is likely to be lost or hurt. You can prevent your dog from wandering by keeping him chained or by fencing him in. But the first technique is not much fun for your dog and the second technique can be very expensive. A better solution is to teach your dog not to leave your property unless you are with him.

Training Equipment: Choke collar, six-foot lead, and a three- to five-foot twig from a live tree. The twig should have some leaves at the end.

Training Period: Three or four 10-minute sessions per day for about one week.

Desired Result: When your dog has responded to the training, you can be confident that he will remain on your property—even when he is able to leave.

The purpose of this training is to make your dog recognize your property line as a boundary that he may not cross. To accomplish this, walk your dog along the property lines from corner to corner. Keep him on leash and in the heel position. Every ten to fifteen feet you should stop and then resume walking. As you do this, make sure that you are a few inches off your property, but that your dog does not step over the property line. If he starts to do this, there are three ways to correct him:

(1) Scold him by saying "no" and "shame."

(2) Jerk the lead.

(3) Use the branch to tap his front legs in the vicinity of his knees.

These three corrective measures should be applied at the same time.

When you reach the end of your property, make a 180° turn. Now you and your pet are both on your grounds, but your pet should be closer to the outside edge. Continue walking along the property lines. If your pet steps over, correct him by using the three techniques.

After three or four days, you should be able to drop the lead on the ground and still practice with your dog. If while you are doing this he starts to stray, keep him from going off the property by stepping on the leash. When your dog has demonstrated that he will stay on the property even though you are not holding the lead, you can remove the lead altogether. Continue to practice until you are confident. Then test your pet by observing him from a point that is far removed from your property. If he tries to leave your grounds, scold him and order him back. If he remains on your land, you know that your training has been successful.

RUNNING AWAY: Suppose you are out with your dog and he runs away from you—how should you react? If you try to catch him, you will only succeed in getting out of breath and amusing whoever happens to be watching. A better idea is to pause for a moment and evaluate the situation.

Your dog has been living in your home and eating your food for as long as he can remember. He is not likely to jeopardize his place in your household by running away and getting lost. What he is doing is having a little fun at your expense.

To regain control, turn around and pretend that you are leaving. Walk slowly so that your dog can catch up with you and call his name while you are walking. If you convince him that you are on your way home, he is likely to hurry up and join you.

As your dog approaches, you may be tempted to scold him or hit him, but both of these temptations should be resisted. Your dog should not be punished for returning to your side. However, he has violated his freedom and, because of this, it must be taken away.

If he has been walking free, you will have to put him back on lead. If the lead has been on but has been trailing on the ground, you will have to pick it up and hold it tight.

STAIRS, CLIMBING: Since dogs are agile creatures, you might not expect them to need help in learning how to use the stairs. For large breeds step climbing seems natural, but for smaller dogs getting up and down may be a problem. If your dog requires assistance, put him on a lead and coax him onto the first step. Then turn him so he is facing the landing and tug the lead gently to help him down. Repeat this procedure a few times and then try moving your dog to the second step.

If your dog continues to be successful, keep advancing him one step at a time and eventually remove the lead. Stair training, like other types of instruction, may require patience. If your dog does not respond quickly, keep him away from the steps for a few days. When you resume training start with the first step and gradually work your way up.

TRAINING SESSIONS: Problems with training sessions are not uncommon. Many handlers complain that when they work with their dogs the time seems to drag or the dog seems listless or disinterested. To avoid having these experiences you may find it helpful to remember the acronym ALOFT. This indicates that in planning training sessions it is important to consider A for "area," L for "length," O for "often," F for "fun" (not "frustration"), and T for "timing."

Area. Your training sessions will have to be held in an area where there is enough room to perform the exercises. In choosing a place, you will also have to consider the surroundings. Don't try to train your dog next to a baseball field or he will pay more attention to the game than he does to you.

Length. There is no rule saying how long you should practice, but it is common knowledge that several short sessions are more productive than one long one.

Often. Until a dog is really proficient, he will have to practice an exercise several times until he has mastered it. For the beginning dog, one practice session a week is not enough. It is better to work with him every day if you have the time.

Fun (not Frustration). For the sake of the dog and handler, training sessions should not be drudgery. Constant praise and an occasional treat will make your dog perform better. It is also a good idea to mix your exercises. Don't devote an entire training session to new material; follow a difficult routine with an exercise that your dog has already learned. The last exercise of the day should be one that you can perform successfully.

Timing. The worst time to work with your dog is after he has had a big meal and is full and lazy. If your dog seems sluggish, you will have to decide whether he just needs some prodding or whether it is better to work with him at another time.

VISITORS, ANNOYING OF: Some people feel that their homes are not big enough for their guests and their pets. This is because their visitors are often greeted by an angry-looking dog who barks at them and pounces on top of them. If this type of behavior continues, an otherwise well-behaved dog may be put up for adoption.

If you experience this problem, don't get rid of your pet. First try to train him with the following technique.

Training Equipment:	Choke collar and six-foot leash. Cheap water pistol and a strong white vinegar solution.
Training Time:	Two or three sessions a day until the habit is corrected.
Desired Result:	People who are welcome in your home will be able to visit without being annoyed by your dog.

This exercise requires at least one other person to play the role of the visitor. When training begins, you and your dog should be inside the house about three feet from the main entrance. Your dog should be on lead and should be sitting in the heel position.

At a signal from you, the visitor will either knock on the door or ring the door bell. This is where the training begins. If the dog starts to bark or leaves his sitting position, you should correct him in three ways:

(1) Scold him by saying "no" and "shame."

(2) Firmly jerk the lead and return the dog to the sitting position.

(3) Squirt a small amount of the vinegar solution in the dog's mouth.

Wait until the dog has settled down and then instruct the visitor to either knock or ring the doorbell again. This time the dog should have no reaction; he should remain seated and should not bark. If the dog behaves, ask the visitor to knock or ring the bell three more times. If there is no bad response, the visitor may come in.

When the visitor enters, the dog should behave just as he did when this person was outside. If there is any deviation, the three corrective measures should be used. Sometimes the combination of these three deterrents is not enough. The dog will continue to pounce on the person coming in the door. When this happens, the visitor must discourage this behavior by lifting his or her right knee and thrusting it firmly into the dog's chest.

Once the proper response has been learned, practice should continue for a few days until you are sure that the dog understands what you want. In working with your dog, there are two additional points that you should keep in mind.

(1) The chest and water gun punishment should not be too severe, because you should be willing to tolerate a small amount of barking. This is important if there is a suspicious stranger in the vicinity of your home.

(2) Every time your dog performs correctly, he should be praised. This will keep your dog happy and will help you cut down on the training time.

WALKING YOUR DOG: The heeling exercises will make your dog an obedient companion when you go for walks. Usually, the command "heel" and a firm tug on the leash are all that you need to keep your dog from forging ahead of you or lagging behind. However, if your dog fails to heed these signals, there is another action that you can take. Hold the stem of the leash with your left hand and twirl the loose end with your right. If your dog persists in forging or lagging, tap him on the nose with the loose end of the leash.

After your dog has been corrected in this way a few times, he will learn to respond to the twirling motion that precedes the punishment. When this happens, just a gesture with the loose end of the leash will be enough to make your dog behave.

Index